D0467701

FIFTY PLACES TO GO

BIRDING BEFORE YOU DIE

FIFTY PLACES TO
GO BIRDING
BEFORE YOU DIE

**Birding Experts Share
the World's Greatest Destinations**

Chris Santella

Foreword by Bill Thompson, III

STEWART, TABORI & CHANG · NEW YORK

Published in 2007 by Stewart, Tabori & Chang
An imprint of Harry N. Abrams, Inc.

Text copyright © 2007 by Chris Santella

Photograph credits: Pages 2, 26, 60, 138, 158, 188, 194, and 219: © David Dvorak, Jr.; pages 10, 74, 134, 164, and 184: © Arthur Morris/BIRDS AS ART; pages 12 and 206: © Steve Rooke/Sunbird; pages 16 and 168: © Brian O'Keefe; page 20, 66, and 150: © Scott J. Hein/www.heinphoto.com; page 28: © Mark Godfrey/The Nature Conservancy; page 36: © Ian Montgomery; page 44: © K. David Bishop; page 48: © Calvin Ng/www.photokk.com; page 56: © Bill Schmoker; page 70: © Ralph Paonessa/RPPhoto.com; page 78: © José Illanes; page 82: © Bryan Bland; pages 92 and 108: © Tim Gallagher; page 96: © Bill Thompson, III; page 100: © Bob Sundstrom; page 104: © János Oláh/Sakertour (www.sakertour.hu); page 114: © Peter P. Marra; page 120: © Nick Garbutt/Indri Images; page 124: © Paul J. Garrity; page 130: © Joe Keenan/The Nature Conservancy; page 142: © Lloyd Spitalnik; page 146: © T. Douglas Rodda; page 154: © Ben Muskin/The Nature Conservancy; page 172: © Tim Laman; page 179: © Steve Mulligan; page 198: © Roger Neckles/www.rogerneckles.com; page 214: © www.operationmigration.org

All rights reserved. No portion of this book may be reproduced, stored in a retrieval system, or transmitted in any form or by any means, mechanical, electronic, photocopying, recording, or otherwise, without written permission from the publisher.

Library of Congress Cataloging-in-Publication Data
Santella, Chris.
Fifty places to go birding before you die : birding experts share the
world's greatest destinations / by Chris Santella.
p. cm.
ISBN 978-1-58479-629-9
1. Bird watching–Guidebooks. I. Title.

QL677.5.S27 2007
598.072'34–dc22
2007021503

Printed and bound in China
10 9 8 7 6 5 4 3 2 1

HNA
harry n. abrams, inc.
a subsidiary of La Martinière Groupe

115 West 18th Street
New York, NY 10011
www.hnabooks.com

CONTENTS

ACKNOWLEDGMENTS

This book would not have been possible without the assistance of the expert birders who shared their time and experiences to help bring these fifty great birding venues to life. Birders—the "fraternity and sorority of the field glass," to paraphrase Roger Tory Peterson—are a most pleasant and generous group of people, and I hope to spend more time with them in the future. To these men and women, I offer the most heartfelt thanks. I would especially like to thank Debi Shearwater, who offered much advice and countless introductions to her vast circle of birding peers. Likewise, I'd like to thank Stephanie Meeks of the Nature Conservancy, Phil Eager of the Sierra Club, and Jan Pierson of Field Guides, who also made many introductions on my behalf, and Bryan Bland, Peter Marra, Kenn Kaufman, and Bill Thompson, III, who inspired me with their tales from the field and their willingness to educate a nonbirder. I also want to acknowledge the fine efforts of my editors Jennifer Levesque and Kate Norment, designer Galen Smith, and copyeditors Sylvia Karchmar and Elizabeth Norment, whose efforts were instrumental in bringing this book into being. Thanks should also go to my agent, Stephanie Kip Rostan, who always provides sage counsel. The list of thanks would hardly be complete without a nod to my mom and dad, who encouraged me to pursue my dream of being a writer . . . and most of all to my wife, Deidre, and daughters, Cassidy Rose and Annabel Blossom, who have again and again displayed tremendous patience, flexibility, and love.

FOREWORD

Why is it that we humans admire birds so much? Is it their dazzling plumage? Is it their ethereal, musical song? How about their courtship rituals and devotion to mate and offspring? These are all admirable explanations for our love of birds, but I think it's even more simple than that. After all, birds have been doing something for eons that humans have only figured out in the past hundred years—flying. It's the freedom, the power of the ability to fly that draws us most to birds. They are not bound, as we are, to the ground. Birds ignore the bonds of gravity, and we wish that we could, too. And so we watch birds in wonder and seek them out wherever they occur.

All bird watchers have a birding spot that stands above all others—a place that has delivered unbelievable numbers of birds or even one special individual bird, or perhaps a jaw-slackening variety of species in one memorable wave of activity. These are the sacred places of the birder. We revisit them in person when we can, and we relive our experiences in these beloved places (and hope to replicate them) every time we don our binoculars.

Chris Santella has combed the world of birding for fifty of the "must-bird" places on planet Earth. He's gathered nominations of locations from some of the most intrepid and well-traveled among the tribe of feather-questing aficionados: professional birders, tour leaders, authors, artists, and ornithologists. Birdy places near and far are represented, from Guatemala to North Dakota to Greenland, from Point Reyes to Hawk Mountain to Cley Next the Sea to Kazakhstan to Borneo and Papua New Guinea. In *Fifty Places to Go Birding Before You Die*, Chris Santella has given us a treasure map to the best birding places in the world.

Bird watching has been my personal and professional focus for more than thirty years and it's been good to me. Many of the most enduring friendships of my life have started with the chance meeting of a fellow birder in the field. After all, bird watchers are among the most likeable, friendliest people you'll ever meet. I encourage you to stop what you're doing, right now, grab your binoculars, go outside, and find some birds. Better yet, plan a trip to one of these fifty places. You'll be sure to find lots of great birds, and, I'll wager, an equal number of great people.

Bill Thompson, III
Editor, Bird Watcher's Digest

INTRODUCTION

I have several fly-fishing friends who also are interested in birds, and I got my first sense of how strong the pull of birding can be while on the river some years ago. I can recall an occasion when, after a long morning of very few bites, the fishing suddenly turned on. After landing a few sassy trout, I turned around to see how my buddies were doing upriver, and they were nowhere to be found. When I caught up with them later, I asked why they'd left just as the fishing was getting good. "We heard some warblers," they said, "and we wanted to see them." Warblers over rising trout?

Apparently so!

While I cannot yet count myself an avid birder, I've gotten to know a few over the years. I'm fascinated by the different perspectives on the pastime—from the ardent big-lister on a constant quest for new species to the amateur naturalist who can be content watching one family of birds for hours on end. Though their motivations and pacing are varied, most birders I know share a common trait—a desire to see new birds in new places, to collect new experiences as well as observations of new species.

For these people, I was inspired to write Fifty Places to Go Birding Before You Die.

"What makes a place you have to bird before you die?" you might ask. The presence of rare or unfamiliar birds? Many birds? Incredible scenery? Incredible ecosystems? Other birders? The answer would be all of the above, and an abundance of other criteria. One thing I knew when I began this project—I was not the person to assemble this list. So I followed a recipe that served me well in my first three Fifty Places books—to seek the advice of some professionals. To write Fifty Places to Go Birding Before You Die, I interviewed a host of people closely connected with the birding world and asked them to share some of their favorite experiences. These experts range from professional birders (like Kenn Kaufman and Bret Whitney) to ornithologists (like John Fitzpatrick and Pamela Rasmussen) to conservation organization executives (like Steve McCormick and Carter Roberts) to journalists and wildlife artists (like Bill Thompson, III and Julie Zickefoose). Some spoke of <u>venues</u> that are near and dear to their hearts, places where they've built their professional reputations; others spoke of places they've only visited once, but that made a profound impression. People appreciate birding for many different reasons, and this range of attractions is evidenced here. (To give a sense of the breadth of interviewees' birding backgrounds, a bio of each individual is included after each essay.)

OPPOSITE:
A Semipalmated
Sandpiper enjoys a
drink—and, perhaps,
its reflection.

While this book collects fifty great birding experiences, it by no means attempts to rank the places discussed, or the quality of the experiences afforded there. Such ranking is, of course, largely subjective—an open-sea adventure for pelagic enthusiasts might prove anathema for someone with a fondness for songbirds . . . and dry land. In this spirit, venues are listed alphabetically by state or country.

In the hope that a few readers might embark on their own adventures, I have provided some "If You Go" information at the end of each chapter, including the names of reputable tour companies that lead birding-oriented trips to the venue in question. The "If You Go" information is by no means a comprehensive list, but should give would-be travelers a starting point for planning their trip.

One needn't travel to the ends of the earth to have a rewarding birding experience. Yet a trip to a dream venue can create memories for a lifetime. It's my hope that this little book will inspire you to embark on some new birding adventures of your own.

OPPOSITE:
Birders take aim in the Tien Shan mountains of Kazakhstan.

THE DESTINATIONS

Alaska

ARCTIC NATIONAL WILDLIFE REFUGE

RECOMMENDED BY **Bob Dittrick**

The Gray-headed Chickadee is one of the most difficult North American resident species to observe. Bob Dittrick has cracked the mystery of uncovering this little bird. Along the way, he's helped birders understand the grandeur of one of the world's last great wilderness tracts.

"I was initially drawn to the Arctic National Wildlife Refuge for its tremendous beauty," Bob began, "though I was always looking for birds. I did a number of trips up there—we'd get flown in to do a river trip, set up camp, and often split up and do day hikes to explore. On one trip, I was there with a group of hard-core birders and writers. Back at camp while doing the daily birdlist, one group said they'd seen a Boreal Chickadee. Since this was an unprecedented sighting, we went to have a look the next day, and it turned out that we'd come across a nesting Gray-headed Chickadee (also known as Siberian Tit). Previously, the only place where this bird could be accessed by birders had been on a gravel bar of a river in the western part of Alaska. However, the gravel bar had been washed out, and the bird had not been seen for several years. We were fifty miles north of timberline—not really considered their habitat. As it turned out, the birds were nesting in small poplars. The Gray-headed Chickadee is a pretty tough bird for hard-core listers to come by, so I began leading more trips into the area, as there were a lot of people who wanted to see it. The past few years, we've shifted over to a raft trip. This allows us to hit two proven nesting areas, thus improving our odds."

If Alaska is America's last great wilderness outpost, then the Arctic National Wildlife Refuge (ANWR) is Alaska's most dramatic example of untrammeled nature. ANWR comprises a South Carolina–size chunk of northeastern Alaska, abutting northwesternmost British Columbia to the east and the Beaufort Sea to the north, and bifurcated by the eastern edge of the Brooks Range. Of its nineteen million acres, nearly eight million are designated wilderness. (By definition, designated wilderness regions are roadless; the only way to get in is by foot, plane, or boat.) The

OPPOSITE:
A permanent resident (along with the Gray-headed Chickadee) of ANWR, Willow Ptarmigan (shown in summer plumage) blend in well with their surroundings.

17

topography ranges from alpine (four of the tallest peaks in the Brooks Range are here) to tundra, creating a full range of arctic and sub-arctic ecosystems. A survey of this vast land, which at times is stark, reveals the richest variety of flora and fauna in the circumpolar north, including all three species of North American bears, a huge caribou herd, the northernmost populations of Dall sheep and year-round resident musk oxen.

The Gray-headed Chickadee is one of 194 different bird species that have been recorded in ANWR, according to U.S. Fish and Wildlife Service counts. Each spring and summer, ANWR will see migrants arriving from as far away as South America, with species ranging from Golden Eagles and Gyrfalcons to Tundra Swans and Northern Shrike. The Gray-headed Chickadee is a permanent resident, favoring the willow brush that's sometimes found along the rivers draining the Brooks Range, flowing north to the Beaufort Sea.

Like many species-specific ventures, the quest for the Gray-headed Chickadee would not be characterized as relaxing. "I like to call it a blitz," Bob said. "We cover a lot of ground quickly to improve our odds of success." The trip starts with a bush-plane flight to an area of tundra bench near the river where Bob and his fellow guides have had success. The adventure really begins after the raft and equipment have been portaged a quarter mile to the river. "Often, the river will be frozen in these upper stretches, and we'll have to sled the rafts down a ways. Even once we hit water, there's still a good deal of ice; sometimes it feels like you're going through an ice canyon. I make sure people are well trained about what to do if we encounter a problem on the river. Likewise, I want people to know how to respond to the bears, as there's the potential to come upon them at any time. This is a real wilderness adventure, and we try to be ready for anything.

"There are two spots along the river—a valley and a canyon—where we focus our efforts. In one of the spots where we'd seen the bird in the past, there were no trees. I had a theory that the chickadees were using old swallows' nests in the cliffs. This turned out to be correct." In ten years of leading Gray-headed Chickadee blitzes, Bob has come up empty only once.

While the challenge of finding a rare species like the Gray-headed Chickadee can be extremely rewarding, the real appeal of an expedition to the Arctic National Wildlife Refuge extends beyond birding. "A few years ago," Bob continued, "we were hiking upriver, heading for the take-out. We'd found the birds a day earlier, and everyone in the group was in good spirits. We had paused on a knoll above a pond, as a grizzly bear was working the hillside in the direction we needed to go; we decided it would be a good time to sit back and watch birds until he moved along. As we were sitting there, a wolf came up from the other side of the knoll. It came within fifty feet of the group; it was really checking us out. One of the members of the party said, 'Jeez, we're surrounded by carnivores!'"

BOB DITTRICK is co-owner of Wilderness Birding Adventures (www.wildernessbirding.com), based in Eagle River, Alaska. He began birding during graduate school in the late 1960s. While working as a naturalist for Fairfax County Parks in Virginia during the 1970s, Bob encountered the bird migration at Cape May, New Jersey. He banded birds at Cape May for many years before quitting his job to help launch the Cape May Bird Observatory. He then headed to Oregon State University where he taught interpretation. In 1978, Bob moved to Alaska, where he became the chief of interpretation and education for Alaska state parks. In 1986, he launched Wilderness Birding Adventures to combine his passions of birding, environmental education, and adventuring in the wilderness. When not out guiding, running a business, or banding raptors from a ridgetop camp during Alaska's fall hawk migration, Bob is likely skijoring to a remote cabin, checking and maintaining nearly a hundred owl nest boxes, or discovering international travel.

IF YOU GO

► **Getting There:** Most trips to the Arctic National Wildlife Refuge will stage in Fairbanks, Alaska, which is primarily served by Alaska Airlines. From here, your outfitter will arrange a charter flight into ANWR.

► **Best Time to Visit:** The window for visiting ANWR is mid-June to late August. Sometimes the season is longer, though these dates are most reliable.

► **Guides/Accommodations:** Wilderness Birding Adventures (907-694-7442; www.wilderness birding.com) leads at least one Gray-headed Chickadee float trip each summer season; this past year's trip was in June.

Alaska

GAMBELL

RECOMMENDED BY **John W. Fitzpatrick**

"I've birded in most parts of the world," John Fitzpatrick recalled. "Of the places I've been, there's no place that has so utterly captivated me and changed my life as Gambell."

For Big Listers, Gambell, on St. Lawrence Island, is a must-visit spot, at least in part because of the potential to spot rare Asian migrants that can't be found with any reliability anywhere else in North America. The appearance of these species is not surprising, as St. Lawrence Island rests in the Bering Sea, much closer to Kamchatka and the Chukchi Peninsula than it does to the Alaskan mainland (distance to Russia—approximately 40 miles; distance to Nome—200 miles). Gambell and St. Lawrence have been the home of Alaskan and Siberian Yup'ik (Eskimo) people for thousands of years. Gambell takes its name from a missionary family from Iowa who came to St. Lawrence for several years in the 1890s, and who perished after a trip to the mainland when their ship sank in a storm. The Gambells—and for that matter, other mainland visitors—have had little impact on the Yup'ik way of life. Most Gambell residents are subsistence hunters, living on whale, walrus, seal, and birds. One aspect of modern life that some islanders have adopted is the ATV, which is ideal for traversing St. Lawrence Island's notoriously difficult-to-negotiate pea gravel; enterprising residents will convey visiting birders around the island for a modest fee.

"My trip to Gambell was in early June of 1993," John continued, "after an American Ornithologists' Union meeting in Fairbanks. It was a tour put together by Kenn Kaufman. We started in Nome with a day's drive up the Kougarok Road—certainly one of the most unbelievable birding roads anywhere. There were Gyrfalcons on the cliffs, and we also came upon Bluethroats and Arctic Warblers—a birding experience unique to the spot. At the end of the mainland, we left the car and battled our way up a muddy, lump-filled hill in search of Bristle-thighed Curlew, as they were known to nest in the area. Several people in our party couldn't make the walk, but the hardy survivors were treated to the rare curlews, flying about, calling and landing. Whimbrel were

OPPOSITE:
Sivuqaq Mountain,
on St. Lawrence
Island, sometimes a
resting spot for
Eurasian Dotterel.

also present farther down the hill. All this on a sunny, far northern Arctic day.

"Though for me, even this dreamlike experience did not hold a candle to Gambell."

It was not the rare species found at Gambell that had such a profound impression on John. Instead, it was the sheer magnitude of the bird life he encountered there. "When we got out to the pebbly beach that's the preferred vantage point for seabirds, there were a million birds—and I'm not exaggerating—a teeming horde of murrelets, auklets, murres, ducks, geese, loons, and the occasional shorebird flock. This experience goes on for twenty-four hours. It gets windy out on the shore, and we built a little lean-to with some driftwood and plywood that we found to get a bit of shelter. I remember being out there at midnight, enduring the wind. There were just enough rare things coming by that you'd never want to go to bed; there was the intermittent rein-forcement of an Emperor Goose, a Yellow-billed Loon, a Spectacled Eider. All of this against a constant backdrop of 300,000 to 1,000,000 seabirds, zipping back and forth from their nesting colonies to the sea to feed, then back again. For me, Gambell provided a moving image of what the earth used to be before humans got here. Here you can still experience the teeming biologi-cal world in its full biomass. List-building aside, I'd love to get people there simply to get a sense of this spectacular biomass."

It's safe to say that one does not visit Gambell for its upscale accommodations. "We stayed in a little beat-up house—no toilet, no running water," John said. "Fortunately, you don't spend too much time inside, as it never gets dark in June." Some of the hotspots are less than romantic, at least in name. The boneyards—which are the final resting places for the remains of the vil-lagers' marine mammal prey—are a haven for vagrant passerines, like Eurasian Bullfinch and Common Cuckoo. Gambell's boatyard and trash dumps are other popular spots. Asiatic shore-birds can sometimes be spied on a lake and its accompanying marshes a short distance from town. The cliffs that run from Sivuqaq Mountain to the sea host multitudes of nesting alcids; vis-itors will have an excellent chance to see Dovekie. If the snow on the mountain is not too fore-boding, some will hike up for a chance to spy Eurasian Dotterel, a plover that will sometimes appear on St. Lawrence Island.

Considering Gambell's reputation for Asian rarities, there's a chance that visitors could not only come upon a lifebird for their own list, but a bird that's never been seen in North America. Perhaps that thought was going through John Fitzpatrick's mind one foggy afternoon during his brief Gambell visit. "I was down near the garbage dump, and saw a little finch-type thing. I got my glasses on it, thinking it was going to be a rare Siberian species. It was a finch, sure enough, with a big bill, a black bib, and a chestnut crown. I almost did a double take when I realized it was a freakin' House Sparrow. It was my only disappointment at Gambell, although it was only the second record for the species in Alaska!"

JOHN W. FITZPATRICK has been the director of the Cornell Lab of Ornithology and a professor of ecology and evolutionary biology at Cornell University since 1995. Previously he was director of Florida's Archbold Biological Station and curator of birds at Chicago's Field Museum. He has led scientific expeditions to remote areas of South America and published extensively on tropical species, including seven new bird species he discovered. John was coleader of the Ivory-billed Woodpecker search effort for the 2004–2005 season when the bird was rediscovered in Arkansas. He received his Ph.D. from Princeton University and A.B. from Harvard University.

IF YOU GO

➤ **Getting There:** Gambell is generally reached via Nome, and is served by Bering Air. You can reach Nome via Anchorage on Alaska Airlines.

➤ **Best Time to Visit:** Late May/early June is the prime time for visiting Gambell.

➤ **Guides:** A number of birding tour companies lead trips to Gambell, including Wings (888-293-6443; www.wingsbirds.com); Victor Emanuel Nature Tours (800-328-8368; www.ventbirds.com) and Wilderness Birding Adventures (907-694-7442; www.wildernessbirding.com.)

➤ **Accommodations:** Beds are limited in Gambell. Should you go it alone, one option is the Sivuqaq Inn (907-985-5335).

SOUTHEASTERN ARIZONA

RECOMMENDED BY **Terry E. Moore**

"As part of my role with Leica, I've gotten to travel to many exotic birding locales," Terry Moore began. "Southeastern Arizona stands out for me on many levels. It's a completely different environment than where I live in the southeastern United States, and offers dramatically different habitats—desert and canyon terrain, as you might expect in Arizona, but also riparian woodlands, sky islands, and even Hudsonian spruce forests. There's so much geographic diversity, you don't have to go to the same kind of place two days in a row. Such a wide variety of habitat gives rise to tremendous species diversity. There are many specialty birds that are common to the region. And thanks to its proximity to Mexico, there's always the opportunity to come upon neotropic accidentals, like Aztec Thrushes and Flame-colored Tanagers."

Say "southeastern Arizona" in birding circles, and eyes are likely to sparkle and involuntary smiles likely to spread across assembled faces. Names like Patagonia Rest Area, Cave Creek Canyon, Ramsey Canyon, and California Gulch are etched in gold leaf in the Where's Where of American birding. When casual "Christmas Count–only" birders begin to take their pastime more seriously and eventually come to plan their first full-fledged birding vacation, many will set their sights on Tucson and points due south and east. From a birding perspective, southeastern Arizona loosely implies the corner of the state cordoned off by Interstate 19 to the west, Highway 10 to the north, Mexico to the south, and New Mexico to the east. Here, several mountain ranges—the Huachucas, the Mules, and the Chiricahuas, to name a few—rise from the surrounding deserts and grasslands, providing a meeting ground for northern birds moving south and subtropical species reaching their northern boundaries. Some of this sky-island habitat is home to flora and fauna found nowhere else in the world.

"I don't think I'll ever forget my first trip to southeastern Arizona, as I found my 500th ABA life bird," Terry added. "I think I got about fifty new species on that trip. Any expectations that I might have had before going were exceeded; though I should add that I didn't have an abundance of preconceptions. I didn't review background materials a great deal before going, as it was first and foremost a business trip. And I figured there would be enough people at the ABA convention I was attending who knew the area well, and would be willing to have me tag along or at least pick their brains. Since that first visit, I've done a good deal of exploring. It's worth noting that for the birder who wants to go it alone, southeastern Arizona has a very well-developed infrastructure. Locations are clearly identified, well-documented, and reasonably easy to get to. It was very surprising to me how accessible everything was. I could sit down with one of the regional birding guides, and if I wanted to see a Red-faced or Rufous-capped Warbler, a Five-striped Sparrow, or a Ruddy Ground Dove, I could do so. On the other hand, if you have limited time and are looking to build a list, there's a great group of guides in the area." (It's not a surprise that many of birding's great luminaries call the greater Tucson region home when they're not traveling the world.)

There are interesting things going on in southeastern Arizona almost any time of the year, though those hoping to observe the greatest number of the region's signature species will optimize their chances by visiting between mid-April and mid-September. Though summer temperatures can be taxing, July and August visits can be very worthwhile. "Most non-birders would think you're crazy to visit Arizona in July or August, but the late-summer rainy season is one of the most rewarding for hummingbirds," Sherri Williamson and Tom Wood, codirectors of the Southeastern Arizona Bird Observatory, have written. "Fall migration begins as early as late June with the arrival of the first southbound Rufous Hummingbirds, and peaks between late August and mid-September." (The region generally records at least thirteen different hummingbird species each year.)

Of the many "rare" species that draw birders to southeastern Arizona, one standout is the Elegant Trogon. Brilliant metallic red and green, this bird is strikingly beautiful, rivaling the appeal of its cousin, the Resplendent Quetzal. The bird's brilliant visual appeal is made more endearing by its somewhat less beguiling call, a barking croak that will not be easily confused with other avian life forms. There are several spots in the region where you have decent odds of coming upon Elegant Trogon during spring and summer breeding months, though your best bet is Cave Creek Canyon, in the Chiricahuas. This area boasts the largest population in the United States—and many consider it the region's most beautiful and prolific birding spot.

Most everyone who's done a bit of birding enjoys showing other people birds that they haven't seen. A big part of the pleasure derived comes from the very act of sharing, which is such a significant facet of the birding ethos. And a little, one must admit, comes from the opportunity

to show off. Sometimes the act of sharing has rewards one might not have even expected, and these are the best rewards of all. "I was birding at Beatty's Guest Ranch and Orchard in a little canyon near Sierra Vista, with some younger birders, age eleven to fifteen or sixteen," Terry recalled, "There is a tremendous variety of hummingbirds in the region—I've seen as many as ten species in a day. These kids had never been to Beatty's before. To see the expressions of joy and wonder on their faces as they were presented with the spectacle of all of these hummingbirds—not just one or two species, but seven or eight, and maybe sixty individual birds—was a revelation to me. I think that adults sometimes forget that wonder. For us, it becomes black and white—'Yeah, I saw it, it was nice, it was pretty.' Those children's expressions of wonder as they tried to sort things out were something to take away, a tremendous thing."

TERRY E. MOORE has had a lifelong interest in the outdoors. After military service, Terry began a career in the consumer photographic industry. He helped launch Leica Camera's (www.leica-camera.us) Sport Optics Division in 1995, a perfect complement to his interest in birding, nature observation and hunting; he serves as the vice president of the division today. Terry recently tallied his 700th ABA Area Life Bird—a Yellow-browed Warbler on Attu. Terry currently resides in Roswell, Georgia, with Judy, his wife of forty-two years. They both enjoy spending time with their two adult children and three grandchildren.

OPPOSITE:
An Elegant Trogon, one of southeast Arizona's "hope-to-see" birds.

IF YOU GO

➤ **Getting There:** Most birders visiting southeastern Arizona will fly into Tucson, which is served by most major carriers.

➤ **Best Time to Visit:** There's something going on here most of the year. Late April to mid-May is a favorite time for observing migrants and specialties. Fall migration peaks in early- to mid-September. Visit the Southeastern Arizona Bird Observatory website (www.sabo.org) for details.

➤ **Guides:** There are many birding guides in the region, including Hi Lonesome Bird Tours (800-743-2668; www.hilonesome.com).

➤ **Accommodations:** A few southeastern Arizona birders' favorites include Ramsey Canyon Inn (520-378-3010; www.ramseycanyoninn.com), Beatty's Guest Ranch & Orchard (520-378-2728), and Southwestern Research Station (520-558-2396). The Metropolitan Tucson Convention and Visitors Bureau (www.visittucson.org) has a comprehensive list of accommodations in the region.

BIG WOODS

RECOMMENDED BY **Allan Mueller**

Few events have rocked the birding world as much as the report from an amateur naturalist named Gene Sparling on February 11, 2004, about a large and unusual woodpecker he spotted while paddling his kayak on Bayou DeView in the Cache River National Wildlife Refuge in eastern Arkansas. A stealth team of A-list ornithologists soon descended upon the Cache River Refuge and the adjoining White River National Wildlife Refuge to the south. After a yearlong search spearheaded by the Cornell Lab of Ornithology and the Nature Conservancy, which yielded a number of fleeting eyewitness accounts, four seconds of video footage were captured. Extensive frame-by-frame analysis led to a press conference (attended by major media outlets) where John Fitzpatrick, director of the Cornell Lab of Ornithology and leader of the project's research team, made the following announcement:

"The bird captured on video is clearly an Ivory-billed Woodpecker. Amazingly, America may have another chance to protect the future of the Ivory-billed Woodpecker and the awesome forests where it lives."

Birding had gone Hollywood. The forest in question is known as the Big Woods.

The Big Woods is the largest remaining corridor of bottomland hardwood forest in the Mississippi Delta (usually a delta is at the mouth of a river, but the historic floodplain of the lower Mississippi River is also called the Delta) north of the Atchafalaya River, adjoining the Mississippi, White, and lower Arkansas rivers, as well as the Cache River and its main tributary, Bayou DeView. The 550,000 acres that comprise the Big Woods are the remnants of a vast tract of big timber wetland forests—nearly 25 million acres of bald cypress, water tupelo, and oak—that once encompassed areas of seven states. "It's the area of the Delta where the upper region begins to give way to the lower," said Allan Mueller. "It's a floodplain that stems from glacial times, and as such, is extremely fertile. The clearing of trees for timber and agricultural purposes has denuded

OPPOSITE:
Once thought
extinct, the elusive
Ivory-billed
Woodpecker is
believed to survive
deep in the swampy
Big Woods.

29

much of the original forest. Dams and channel dredging have changed the seasonal flooding that's so important to these forests. Despite all this, the area around the White and Cache rivers and Bayou DeView is still remarkably productive for wildlife." In addition to the Cache River and White River National Wildlife Refuges, public lands falling in the Big Woods region include the Dagmar Wildlife Management Area, Rex Hancock/Black Swamp Wildlife Management Area, Trusten Holder Wildlife Management Area, Wattensaw Wildlife Management Area, and Benson Creek Natural Area. (Readers of William Faulkner may remember the Big Woods as the scene of his short story The Bear; this story and three others were included in a 1955 collection of hunting tales called Big Woods.)

The Ivory-billed Woodpecker has captivated naturalists from John James Audubon and onward. It's one of the world's largest woodpeckers, and birders' perception of its size is further exaggerated by its loud flying, the result of stiff wing feathers. The Ivory-bill's nickname—the Lord God Bird—is said to have derived from the tendency of those observing it in flight to proclaim, "Lord God, what a bird!" Ivory-bills feed on beetle larvae found in dying hardwoods; their namesake bills (ivory-colored from a layer of keratin over the bill) are ideal for prying away bark to reveal lunch. Ivory-bills once ranged across the southern United States, favoring swampy woods. They were never plentiful, as each pair requires six square miles of forest, but were widespread. Ornithologist James Tanner recorded the decline of Ivory-bills in Louisiana in the 1930s; the last confirmed sighting in the U.S., previous to the recent sighting, was also in Louisiana, in 1944.

The little town of Brinkley, Arkansas, has been positively impacted by the surge of Ivory-bill interest. A flow of visitors has prompted the addition of Ivory-billed Woodpecker burgers at Gene's BBQ, and a modest cottage industry in woodpecker memorabilia. It's also prompted enhancements to the bird's historic habitat. "Since the Ivory-bill's rediscovery, new interpretive trails have been added (or old ones improved) in the refuges with the most promising habitat to take visitors through," Allan continued. "I think the prettiest spots are those that can only be accessed by canoe. One of my favorite spots is Bayou DeView. There are some cypress in there that are 800 years old. I think it's important to note that much of this area that's been protected is the result of monies raised through license fees and taxes paid by duck hunters.

"Not surprisingly, many visitors today go out looking for Ivory-bills. Since the 2005 sightings, we've had a few others, though no photographic evidence. I'm out there every week, and still haven't seen one! But birders do have a good chance of finding Prothonotary Warblers, Swainson's Warblers, and Mississippi Kite. During winter, you'll come upon large flocks of Snow Geese. In the winter, it's a major waterfowl feeding area. And in the southern sections of the White River

Refuge, there are good populations of black bear and even some alligators. Whether or not you see the Lord God Bird, it's still special."

ALLAN MUELLER is Avian Conservation Project Manager with the Nature Conservancy (TNC) in Arkansas, focusing his efforts on the Ivory-billed Woodpecker Recovery project. (Incidentally, TNC has protected more than 18,000 acres of the Big Woods near the Cache River and White River National Wildlife Refuges through new land acquisitions, with the ten-year goal of restoring 200,000 more acres of the Big Woods.) Before joining TNC, he worked for over thirty years with the United States Fish and Wildlife Service. A passionate birder, Allan is past president of the Mississippi Ornithological Society and the Arkansas Audubon Society.

IF YOU GO

▶ **Getting There:** The primary sites for visiting the Big Woods—the Cache River and White River refuges—are a few hours southeast of Little Rock, which is served by most major carriers.

▶ **Best Time to Visit:** As far as scientists know, Ivory-bills are present throughout the year. Late spring and summer are hot and humid; most will find spring and fall the most pleasant time to visit.

▶ **Guides:** Several operators offer birding tours in the Big Woods area, including Paradise Wings (870-734-2030; www.paradisewings.com) and Big Wood Birder's Lodge (501-590-5568).

▶ **Accommodations:** Brinkley, Arkansas, is the unofficial headquarters for Ivory-bill seekers. You'll find a list of lodging options—including The Ivory Billed Inn—at the Brinkley website (www.brinkleyar.com).

BRUNY ISLAND

RECOMMENDED BY **Dr. Tonia Cochran**

Tonia Cochran came to Tasmania and Bruny Island for graduate work in marine biology. She stayed for the birds. "When I came to Tasmania from Melbourne to do field work, I was struck by how plentiful the bird life was," Tonia said. "While I was completing my dissertation, the opportunity arose to work down here. It was the job I couldn't refuse, and I found the means to move down, and chose to live on Bruny."

Tasmania is a large island located 125 miles south of Melbourne, across Bass Strait. This Australian state boasts large tracts of undisturbed land; nearly 40 percent of Tasmania's 26,000 square miles is given over to national parks and World Heritage sites. In addition to the Tasmanian Devil (yes, there really is such a creature, a carnivorous marsupial the size of a smallish dog), Tasmania has many endemic species of flora and fauna found nowhere else. This list includes twelve species of birds: Tasmanian Native Hen, Forty-spotted Pardalote, Scrubtit, Yellow Wattlebird, Strong-billed Honeyeater, Dusky Robin, Green Rosella, Tasmanian Scrubwren, Tasmanian Thornbill, Yellow-throated Honeyeater, Black-headed Honeyeater, and Black Currawong.

As Tasmania is off the southeastern tip of the Australian continent, Bruny Island rests a few miles off the southeastern tip of Tasmania. ("They call Bruny 'the island off an island, off an island'" Tonia quipped.) Accessible only by vehicular ferry from the mainland (or a short flight from Hobart to the Bruny airstrip), Bruny is divided into two parts, north Bruny and south Bruny, that are connected by a narrow spit of land. With habitat ranging from coastal scrub to cool temperate rain forest to both wet and dry eucalyptus woodland, Bruny is in some ways a microcosm of Tasmania. "In ten or fifteen minutes," Tonia continued, "you can be in a different ecosystem. That's certainly one of the great appeals of birding here. You have a very real chance of ticking off Tasmania's twelve endemic species on Bruny, as they are all here in close proximity. I have a 500-

acre property called Inala that I operate as a preserve. On a special day, you might find all twelve endemics at Inala. There are times when we'll go out and all the endemics are lined up to be viewed. My record locating all twelve is two hours!"

Of the endemics found on Bruny, the most notable for Tonia is the Forty-spotted Pardalote, a species threatened with extinction. It's a tiny bird, measuring just 4 inches; its moniker comes from the white dots that cover its black wings. Scientists believe that half of the world's remaining "Forty-spots," as they are affectionately known, live on Bruny Island. Their decline is credited to the destruction of white gum eucalyptus forests, which the birds rely on for food (both insects and manna, a sweet secretion trees produce when attacked by insects). "I do work rehabilitating habitat for Forty-spots," Tonia continued, "growing and planting white gums. I used to grow 2,000 a year from seedlings, and then plant them. I've smartened up a bit now, and work with school groups to arrange big planting days where the kids grow and plant them as school projects. I treasure the restoration work, as it brings all the theories I've studied into play. It's an amazing experience to see the birds bring their newly fledged young to feed on the young white gums that I have planted." Tonia does similar restoration work with blue gum trees on behalf of the Swift Parrot, another endangered species that calls Bruny a seasonal home in the breeding season.

In addition to its twelve endemic species and the Swift Parrot, Bruny is home to a sizable colony of Little Penguins (Eudyptula minor), the smallest of the world's seventeen penguins. Diminutive indeed at sixteen or seventeen inches in height and about two pounds in weight, Bruny's Little Penguin rookery is situated at the isthmus that connects the northern and southern portions of the island. "One can view these little birds returning to their burrows at dusk mainly during the breeding season (August to February) although they can be found here all year-round," Tonia continued. "They share this area with the Short-tailed Shearwater, which visitors can also view in the spring and summer months. Unfortunately, the main road that connects the two parts of the island passes through this area and the penguins often have to cross the road to access their burrows. Despite an oft-photographed sign alerting motorists of their fellow travelers, some of the penguins are hit by vehicles as they frantically attempt to waddle across the road. Ideally we need funding so that we can fence off both sides of the road and provide underpasses through which the penguins can safely access their burrows."

If a birder makes it as far as Bruny, he/she should certainly set aside some time to explore the main island. "Within ten minutes of the capital city of Hobart there is some wonderful bush land with great bird populations," Tonia said. "Within an hour of Hobart is Mount Field National Park, where you can find species such as Pink Robin and the endemic Scrubtit and Black

Currawong." In Southwest National Park (one of Tasmania's World Heritage areas), one has an excellent chance to see the Orange-bellied Parrot—one of the world's rarest and most endangered species, which breeds here in the spring and summer months. "There are now less than 200 left in the wild," Tonia continued, "and this is their only breeding ground. The Tasmanian Parks and Wildlife Department has set up a tagging/feeding station there to observe them. It's a chance to see a special bird amongst incomparably beautiful surroundings. There is also a chance to view the Ground Parrot, one of only a few ground-dwelling parrots in the world there.

"An aspect of Tasmania that's putting it on the birder's map is that some species that are quite rare on the mainland are easier to find here, birds like the Pink Robin, Olive Whistler, in addition to the Swift- and Orange-bellied Parrot. If you had three days to spend in Tasmania, I'd send you to Bruny, Hobart, and Mount Field. With the exception of the Orange-bellied Parrot, you'd be able to cover most of the species you'd want to cover."

DR. TONIA COCHRAN is the owner and lead guide of Inala Nature Tours (www.inala bruny.com.au). After taking her undergraduate degree and Ph.D. in zoology from the University of Melbourne, she was involved in sub-Antarctic and Antarctic research from 1985 to 1996, and has undertaken consulting and contract work for the Australian Antarctic Division in Tasmania since 1990, including participation in several Australian National Antarctic Research Expedition (ANARE) Marine Science voyages to several sub-Antarctic and Antarctic localities. She has also worked in close association with the invertebrate zoology department at the Museum of Victoria. Tonia regularly speaks at venues in Australia and overseas on topics ranging from Antarctica to ecotourism and guiding, threatened-species conservation, and ornithology. Tonia is extremely involved with the conservation of threatened species. She works as an environmental consultant on a number of projects, providing advice on university postgraduate projects to conservation management plans. Tonia is a founding member of the Bruny Island Protection Group and an advocate for the South Bruny National Park. She is also a member of the National Recovery Team for two endangered birds, the Forty-spotted Pardalote and the Wedge-tailed Eagle, and a participant in the Swift Parrot Recovery Program. Committed to promoting a tourism industry that is ecologically sustainable and educational, Tonia is chair of the organization Wildlife Tourism Australia.

IF YOU GO

➤ **Getting There:** Bruny Island is most easily reached via the Tasmanian capital of Hobart, which has regular service from Sydney and Melbourne through Virgin, Jetstar, and Regional Express. There is regular ferry service to Bruny Island from Kettering, about twenty-five miles south of Hobart.

➤ **Best Time to Visit:** Endemics are present the year-round in Tasmania, though September to May is the most popular time to visit.

➤ **Guides:** Dr. Tonia Cochran (+61 36-293-1217; www.inalabruny.com.au) provides tours on Bruny, both on her property, Inala, and on other parts of the island.

➤ **Accommodations:** The Bruny Island Tasmania Information Guide (www.brunyisland.net.au) lists accommodations on the island, including Tonia's guest house at Inala.

CAPERTEE VALLEY

RECOMMENDED BY **Alan McBride**

Sydney is Australia's largest city, and considered by many to be one of the most dynamic cities in the world. Yet within a few hours of its famed Opera House and pristine harbor rests one of Australia's richest birding venues—Capertee Valley. "You can land at the Sydney airport at 6:00 A.M., be at the entrance to Capertee Valley by 8:30 or 9:00 A.M., and have a species list of 120 birds by 5 P.M.," said Alan McBride. "There's a terrific range of birds in Capertee, and for most visitors, they will be all new species. A ride out to Capertee is a great beginning for birders landing in Australia—and a sensational birding day for anyone."

Isolated from other land masses, Australian fauna has developed on its own unique course. The land that has given us platypus and kangaroos also offers up a wonderful array of birds—some 760 recorded species. Of these, over 300 are found only on the continent (with eight families endemic to Australia). Australia is not a small place; it's roughly the size of the continental United States. That nearly 240 bird species have been recorded in Capertee Valley speaks to its productivity. Naturalist Carol Probets attributes Capertee's plentiful bird life to its geography and tree life: "Being both at the eastern limit for a number of inland species, and near the western limit of some of the more typically eastern species means that the diversity is high for an area of its size. The box-ironbark woodland on the valley floor provides especially good habitat for woodland birds, which are declining elsewhere as a result of habitat loss." (Box and ironbark are varieties of eucalyptus.)

Capertee lies about three hours (120 miles) from downtown Sydney, in a region on the eastern flank of the Great Dividing Range that's called the Blue Mountains. The valley is vast—at its entrance it stretches nearly twenty miles across. "You come over the crest of a hill, and there's an immense canyon to the right," Alan described. "It's quite breathtaking." Over the course of twenty miles, it narrows to less than a mile in width. The floor of the valley is a patchwork of grassy fields

OPPOSITE:
Gang Gang
Cockatoos are some-
times encountered in
Capertee Valley.

and stands of eucalyptus. Many trees are draped with mistletoe, which further abets birdlife. The cliffs of the canyon rise to 2,000 feet, providing a dramatic backdrop for a birding excursion. They also provide an added benefit for late-risers, negating the need to be in the field at dawn, as the walls shield the valley from sunlight until a more reasonable hour. The modest level of agriculture in the valley is believed to have benefited birdlife, providing an even greater level of habitat diversity.

The regimen for a day of birding in Capertee is not terrifically rigorous. "While one can get up in the middle of the night and depart from Sydney to be in the valley near dawn, I suggest that visitors spend the night before in the town of Lithgow," Alan continued. "It's less than an hour from the valley, and makes for a more relaxing day. Once we're in the valley, I'll drive along slowly with the windows rolled down. When we hear a bird, we stop the car and try to find it. Oftentimes, a walk of 100 or 200 meters along the road will meet with success. This approach is very easy on folks. A lot of older guests can't walk two miles up hill and dale. At Capertee, you don't have to. We'll bird by car for the twenty miles from the entrance to the valley to the little town of Glendavis at the other end, and most days we'll see 100 species by 2 P.M. If I have a sense of where people are going on the rest of their stay in Australia, I can help them focus on the birds that they're likely to see only in Capertee. More often than not, if we focus on the difficult-to-find birds, we'll spot the more common species along the way." Birds regularly found in Capertee include Southern Whiteface, Red-capped Robin, Plum-headed Finch, and Yellow Thornbills; rarer finds include the Swift Parrot, Turquoise Parrot, Barking Owl, and Gang Gang Cockatoo.

One of the greatest attractions of Capertee is the chance to see the Regent Honeyeater, a passerine of the Meliphagidae family that's endemic to Australia (nearly half of the world's 182 species of honeyeaters call Australia home). In the not-so-distant past, the Regent Honeyeater—marked by black and yellow lacy scalloping on its breast and back, and brilliant yellow patches on its wings—was a common sight along the wooded slopes of the Great Dividing Range, and was not uncommon throughout southern Australia and western Victoria. Clearing of the box and ironbark eucalyptus where the birds forage for nectar and bugs is responsible for their decline. Estimates place populations between 1,000 and 1,500 birds (the bird has been classified as endangered by the Action Plan for Australian Birds 2000). "Capertee is the primary breeding ground for the Regents," Alan said. "They're here for roughly half the year. When they're off the nest, no one knows where they go. Conservation groups have been planting many trees in the valley to encourage the propagation of the Regent Honeyeater. Of course, the trees encourage other birds—parrots and other species of honeyeaters—as well." Places where box and ironbark are flowering are most promising spots for finding a Regent.

Though he leads trips across Australia, Alan never tires of uncovering the wonders of Capertee for his guests. "Every time I'm able to show someone a Regent Honeyeater or Turquoise Parrot, the look on their face is amazing. That look always makes it worthwhile."

ALAN MCBRIDE has been leading birders around Australia, New Caledonia, New Zealand, Papua New Guinea, southeast Asia, and the sub-Antarctic islands of Australia and New Zealand for almost thirty years. He started leading pelagic birding trips from Wollongong and Sydney in 1978, and has since been on more than 850 pelagic trips around the world. Alan organized and led the first full birding group to the sub-Antarctic islands and was a pioneer in organizing bird-tour groups around Australia in the seventies (he's seen over 750 of Australia's birds). He has led or co-led tours for most of the world's major bird-tour companies.

IF YOU GO

➤ **Getting There:** Capertee Valley is approximately three hours west of Sydney, which is served by many major carriers, including Air New Zealand, British Airways, and Qantas.

➤ **Best Time to Visit:** Weather is mild most of the year in Capertee, with January being the wettest month. Regent Honeyeaters are most abundant in the Australian winter, May though September.

➤ **Guides:** Several guides lead tours around Capertee and the Blue Mountains, including Alan McBride (+61 41-941-4860; amcbride1@mac.com) and Carol Probets (+61 24-782-1831; www.bmbirding.com.au).

➤ **Accommodations:** Tourism New South Wales (www.visitnsw.com.au) offers an exhaustive list of lodging options in Sydney. Lithgow Tourism Information (www.lithgow-tourism.com) lists accommodations around Lithgow. Several cabin rentals are available closer to the valley; visit BM Birding (www.bmbirding.com.au) for details.

THE RUINS

RECOMMENDED BY **Sheri Williamson**

For Sheri Williamson, Belize offers up a perfect serving of two passions—birding and archaeology.

"My first visit to Belize was in 1983," Sheri began. "I was a student at the University of Texas/Arlington and a newlywed, and my new husband and I decided we'd take part in a tropical-biology field course based in the southern part of the country. We drove down—quite an adventure in those days. On the ride down, there were many signs for archaeology sites, but we were on a tight schedule—and someone else's schedule. I had gathered all these maps and information on the Maya, but about all I could do was watch as the signs went by. When we returned in 1987, we visited as many sites as we could, and discovered that many of the ruins were wonderful birding spots as well."

Belize may lack the cachet of Costa Rica in some birding circles, but this small nation (formerly known as British Honduras) tucked south of Mexico's Yucatán peninsula and east of Guatemala on the Caribbean is the domain of over 570 species, including Jabiru Stork, Orange-breasted Falcon, and Harpy Eagle. Nearly half the country consists of forest and savanna, still wild enough to sustain populations of jaguar. "I admire the Belizeans' commitment to conservation," Sheri continued. "Of course, that's one of the reasons it's such a great place to bird. The Belize Zoo really helped stimulate the Belizeans' interest and pride in their wildlife and environment. Many city dwellers had little, if any, experience with the wildlife of their own country. The Belize Zoo changed this." The zoo west of Belize City was established in 1983 to provide a home for an assortment of wild animals that had been used in a documentary film project. It has thrived, and by all reports has been successful in one of its missions: to bring the people of Belize closer to the animals that are part of their natural heritage, and encourage them to protect these animals for future generations.

"Each year, there are further improvements to Belize's birding infrastructure—more lodges, more preserves," Sheri continued. "And there are many fine Belizean guides to show the way. In my opinion, there's no excuse for not using native guides. This way, you get the bird perspective from those who live there, which adds an extra dimension. They're intimately familiar with the wildlife on so many levels."

When the words "Belize" and "ruins" are uttered in the same sentence, many people will think of Tikal, which is actually in neighboring Guatemala (though it's often accessed by tourists from the Belize side of the border). Belize has many notable Mayan remnants of its own. "Belize was the heartland of the lowland Maya," Sheri said. "During the classic period, there were seven or eight times more residents than there are today, and the Mayan culture here was not influenced by the Toltec peoples. When you climb up to the top of any of the temples, you'll typically see lots of small to medium hills in the distance. Most of them are unexcavated ruins. The whole country of Belize is a huge archaeological treasure."

There are several characteristics that make ruins excellent birding spots. First, the regions surrounding noteworthy ruins are designated as national parks, and are managed for wildlife as well as cultural assets. This, of course, preserves large stands of avian habitat. Second, there are facets of the ruins themselves that are conducive to birds. "Archaeologists have found that there are higher incidences of certain plant species in ancient Mayan cities," Sheri continued. "They believe that certain 'wild' plants that yielded fruit or had medicinal properties were cultivated around the cities for convenience's sake, inadvertently creating new bird habitats. The temples have also become habitat. At many ruins, Motmots and Jacamars burrow right into unexcavated temple mounds to make nests, as if they were part of the natural landscape. Inside, you'll sometimes find nesting swifts and hummingbirds—as well as geckos, spiders, and other creatures that may seem like they're out of a horror movie but are cool creatures in their own right."

Of Belize's many identified Mayan ruins, Caracol, in the western Cayo district, is the largest and best known. Dating back to 400 A.D., Caracol (Spanish for snail shell, as many such shells were found here) was lost to modernity until the 1920s, when it was rediscovered and excavation began. Restoration work continues today. It rests in the middle of the Chiquibul Rain Forest, most of which has been preserved. "Caracol is in wild country, near the border with Guatemala," Sheri said. "There's hardly any development yet, so it's perfect for some of the area's more vulnerable and demanding species, such as Harpy Eagles. They're almost extinct in Central America, but a wild one was seen near Caracol in 2000, and since 2003 the Peregrine Fund has released a number of captive-bred Harpies at a research station nearby." Harpy Eagles, which frequent lowland forests from southeastern Mexico south to southern Brazil, are among the largest and most powerful eagles in the world. Their talons—nearly the size of grizzly bear claws—are ideally suited for snaring sloths, monkeys, and other prey as they maneuver through the trees.

"One of the special thrills I've had time and time again in Belize is being out at first light and climbing to the top of one of the temples," Sheri reminisced. "It's an amazing thing to experience the forest waking up around you. Hearing the first croak of the first toucan, then others, then the calls of other birds and howler monkeys adding to the chorus."

SHERI WILLIAMSON is codirector (with her husband, Tom Wood) of the Southeastern Arizona Bird Observatory (www.sabo.org), a nonprofit organization dedicated to the conservation of the birds of southeastern Arizona, their habitats, and the diversity of species that share those habitats through research, monitoring, and public education. She and Tom founded SABO after seven and a half years managing the Nature Conservancy's Ramsey Canyon Preserve. Before moving to Arizona, Sheri worked at jobs ranging from artist to zookeeper and volunteered at the Fort Worth Nature Center as a naturalist and wildlife rehabilitator. She and Tom make their home in Bisbee, Arizona; when they're not in the field, they enjoy playing folk music, reading, and gardening.

IF YOU GO

► **Getting There:** The western sections of Belize are best reached via Belize City, which is served by American, Continental, and United Airlines, among others.

► **Best Time to Visit:** Many of the species people come to Belize to see are present most of the year. Most visitors prefer to avoid the summer months, which are quite warm and humid.

► **Guides:** The lodges below generally have excellent guides on staff. A number of birding travel companies, including Field Guides (800-728-4953; www.fieldguides.com) offer tours in Belize.

► **Accommodations:** Duplooy's Lodge (+501-824-3101; www.duplooys.com) and Pine Ridge Lodge (800-316-0706; www.pineridgelodge.com) near Caracol, and Lamanai Outpost Lodge (888-733-7864; www.lamanai.com) near Lamanai, all cater to birders.

BHUTAN

RECOMMENDED BY **David Bishop**

A three-week birding extravaganza in the tiny Himalayan nation of Bhutan is among the most expensive ground-based tours offered by birding travel companies. The fact that the trips offered by some outfits fill up a year and a half in advance speaks to the wonders of the adventure.

"You always hear people say of a place, 'I wish you could have been here forty years ago!'" David Bishop began. "Bhutan is that place. The environment—and the culture—are still tremendously intact. I've been doing field work in Asia for more than thirty years, and Bhutan—which until thirty years ago was all but closed to outsiders—was considered a Shangri-la for birders and other naturalists. I finally got the chance to go in 1994. I've been back once or twice a year ever since. Each time, I'm more beguiled by the place—the serenity, peace, and tranquility. It rejuvenates the soul to be there. I suppose it says a lot that the wellbeing of Bhutan's citizens is measured not by their GNP but by their GNH—Gross National Happiness—a notion that's been championed by the nation's king."

Most Westerners know little about Bhutan (Land of the Thunder Dragon), a tiny country the size of West Virginia that's sandwiched between India to the south and China to the north. That's largely because until the last few decades, tourists were not permitted to visit the kingdom. The restriction on tourists was lifted in 1974, and today, a limited number of visitors is allowed, each paying a tariff of $250–$300 a day (this keeps out the backpacker types who are less likely to contribute to the local economy). Those fortunate enough to make the long journey are not disappointed. The Bhutanese are warm people, still very influenced by Buddhist traditions that seem mystical to the eyes of outsiders; think Tibet, with far fewer visitors and not nearly as many celebrities. And the surroundings are overwhelming. Fortified monasteries guarding ancient temples (dzongs) cling to hillsides, defying gravity, while the towering mountains—including 23,996-foot Jhomolhari, the "Mountain of the Goddess"—reach high into the clouds.

Perhaps this proximity to the heavens helps lend Bhutan its sacred aura.

"Everyone wears traditional Bhutanese clothing, bright-colored fabric that you'll often see being woven on looms," David said. "Many people live closely with their animals, and each spring they herd their yak high up into the mountains to spend the summer grazing on alpine pastures. One day we were settling into camp, and a brother and sister came by with their cows. They were traditionally clad, blowing horns, which, together with an assortment of cowbells jangling and the myriad calls of cuckoos and barbets, echoing off the surrounding hills, was an unforgettable, defining moment. On another occasion, we were birding near Jakar Dzong—a monastery in the Jakar Valley that translates as 'Fortress of the White Bird.' There's a little village in front of the monastery, and the mountains in the background. It was a cloudy day, but a shaft of light pierced through the gray. It was unforgettable."

For birders, Bhutan is quite simply an unexplored paradise. "From a hard-core birder's perspective," David explained, "Bhutan positions you in the Himalayas at a point where this huge mountain range reaches its most southerly point and consequently is wetter and warmer, and the treeline goes higher. There's a classic phrase in a book on the botany of the Himalayas. The writer says, 'as you go eastward in the Himalayas into Bhutan, the flora is simply too diverse for us to handle in one book.' Of course, with floristic diversity comes great avian diversity." Birders embarking on long adventures in Bhutan (most good organized trips are three weeks in length) will go from an elevation of 150 feet above sea level to altitudes of 12,000 or 13,000 feet. Habitat will range from grassy flood plains to lowland forests of Sal trees to rich subtropical forests to deciduous and evergreen montane forests; in fact, nearly 70 percent of Bhutan is blanketed in virgin forest. Some hillsides are adorned with rhododendrons, magnolias, and other wonderful, colorful flowering plants; the towering mountains are ever looming.

"There's very little hunting in Bhutan," David continued, "and there's nowhere in Asia where birds or mammals are so approachable. A few years back, we were walking along Bhutan's main (read only) highway that crosses the country from west to east; we'd gotten out of the coach to look at some birds. It was ten o'clock in the morning, and the bus was fifty yards behind us. Suddenly, there was a leopard on the road. It wasn't put off by us at all. Eventually it wandered up a gulley, flushing a pheasant as it went. On the same road, we've seen Himalayan Black Bears, and male Satyr Tragopans." (The latter is a pheasant distinguished by the brilliance of its star-spangled deep crimson-red plumage.)

As of 2004, 645 bird species had been officially recorded in Bhutan. These include such megacharismatic species as Himalayan Monal, Rufous-necked Hornbill; Wedge-billed and

OPPOSITE:
Dzongs (fortified monastaries), like the Shomgang Dzong, are an added highlight to a birding adventure in Bhutan.

Long-billed Wren-babblers, Fire-tailed Myzornis, Grosbeaks, Rosefinches, Laughing Thrushes, Ibisbills, Beautiful Nuthatches, and the aforementioned Satyr Tragopans. Most experts feel that the ornithological community has only begun to uncover this country's possibilities. "Over the course of the trips I've led, we've discovered almost thirty birds that had never been recorded before in Bhutan," David said. One of David's most profound identifications came on his first trip to Bhutan. "It was our last morning on the Limithang road, and we were in an area surrounded by steep, precipitous slopes. It was rainy and foggy—not ideal conditions. Suddenly all hell lets loose—there were birds everywhere! I heard a call that was unmistakable—Ward's Trogon. No one had ever seen this bird in the field and there had been no records from anywhere in its range for many years. It seemed too good to be true, and to my initial embarrassment I thought I might have miscalled it and that it was a Striated Laughingthrush, which has been known to imitate the call of other birds. But no! In the half-light through the mist, there it was—a stunning male, colored like no other bird, a brilliant deep salmon pink. It was nothing short of an ornithological orgasm."

DAVID BISHOP has spent much of the past thirty years studying the birds and natural history of Asia, in addition to New Guinea and the southwestern Pacific. Once a police officer amid the streets of London's West End, David has emerged as an acknowledged authority on the birds of these exotic regions. He has undertaken a number of expeditions to survey the birds and other wildlife of previously unexplored regions throughout New Guinea (largely together with Jared Diamond) and Asia, resulting in a number of exciting discoveries and rediscoveries including the incomparable Wallace's Standardwing, a bizarre Bird of Paradise. Some of the results of this work, together with observations gained during the Victor Emanuel Nature Tours expeditions he leads, have been published in the scientific and semipopular literature to which David is a regular contributor. David (with Brian Coates) has published A Guide to the Birds of Wallacea (Sulawesi, the Moluccas, and Lesser Sundas); he is currently working on other book projects. David lives with his wife and daughter (his son currently resides in England) in the university town of Armidale, NSW, Australia. David is the Asia-Pacific director for Victor Emanuel Nature Tours, Inc.

IF YOU GO

➤ **Getting There:** Bhutan is not easy to get to; it requires nearly twenty-four hours of flying time from New York (via London, Bangkok, and Calcutta). Once you reach Asia, Druk Air (www.drukair.com.bt) provides service to Bhutan from Calcutta, New Delhi, and Bangkok.

➤ **Best Time to Visit:** Tours are generally scheduled for early spring.

➤ **Guides:** Thanks to the many logistical challenges associated with traveling in Bhutan, most birders making the trek will travel with a tour company. Victor Emanuel Nature Tours (800-328-8368; www.ventbirds.com) has led tours there since 1994. Field Guides (800-728-4953; www.field guides.com) also leads expeditions. A very limited number of spots are available each year.

➤ **Accommodations:** Those traveling on their own should contact Bhutan Tourism Corporation Limited (+975 2-322647, -324045; btcl@druknet.bt) and consult the official government website, www.kingdomofbhutan.com.

8

DESTINATION

DANUM VALLEY

RECOMMENDED BY **Susan Meyers**

Charles Darwin, who saw a bit of the world, called Borneo "one great wild untidy luxuriant hothouse made by nature for herself." Susan Meyers was equally inspired, before even arriving.

"When I was a child, my parents bought me the Time-Life series of the World's Wild Places," Susan began. "It included an especially good volume on Borneo. I looked at those pictures of the rain forest and the birds, and I was utterly captivated. I couldn't wait to make my way there, and in the late nineties, I finally made it. I wasn't disappointed. The nature writer Richard Nelson once wrote 'what makes a place special is the way it buries itself inside the heart, not whether it's flat or rugged, rich or austere, wet or arid, gentle or harsh, warm or cold, wild or tame.' Borneo is buried inside my heart. When I visit, I feel like I've come home. Of the places I visited there, Danum Valley was incredibly impressive. To my mind, it's one of the great places to bird in southeast Asia. The absolute plethora of animals and plants is overwhelming."

Straddling the equator near the center of Indonesia, Borneo is the world's third-largest island, roughly the size of Texas. The island is split among three nations; the southern two thirds are administered by Indonesia, the northern third by Malaysia, with the exception of a small section in the northwest, which is the sovereign state of oil-rich Brunei. Thanks in part to its sultry climate—the "hothouse" referenced by Darwin—Borneo boasts an incomparable level of biodiversity. It's home to over 15,000 known plants, 350 bird species, 220 mammals, and 150 reptiles and amphibians. Known is emphasized, as biologists believe that there could be thousands of additional plant and animal species that have yet to be identified on the island. According to a study published by the World Wildlife Fund, 361 new flora and fauna have been discovered just since 1996. Scientists are currently in a race against logging and other extraction interests to protect a large swath of equatorial rain forest near the center of the island, which has been dubbed the Heart of Borneo. This area is home to poster-worthy endangered animals such as the Bornean

OPPOSITE:
A Banded Pitta at
the Borneo
Rainforest Lodge.

49

Orangutan, Asian Elephant, Sumatran Rhinoceros, Clouded Leopard, and Bornean Gibbon.

Danum Valley is located within the Heart of Borneo region, roughly forty-five miles from the northeastern town of Lahad Datu in the Sabah province. Its 170 square miles make it Malaysia's largest remaining area of virgin undisturbed lowland rain forest. In addition to hosting a healthy representation of Borneo's most noteworthy mammals, Danum is home to some 275 bird species. "You can see all eight species of hornbill, including Rhinoceros and Helmeted Hornbill," Susan continued, "as well as Bornean Bristlehead, Bornean Ground Cuckoo, Great Argus Pheasant, White-fronted Falconet, and a number of endemic Wren-babblers. Some of the Bornean birds have the craziest names—Fluffy-backed Tit-Babblers, Hairy-backed Bulbul, for example. My clients get a kick out of that. My favorite birds in Danum Valley are the Pittas. I think they're the most exciting bird in all of southeast Asia."

The Borneo Rainforest Lodge is the favored base for birders exploring Danum Valley. The lodge offers an extensive trail system, and platforms for canopy viewing. A normal day in Danum for Susan goes something like this: "When you wake up, the gibbons are calling—to my ear, one of the great sounds of the world. We generally arise very early—fiveish—to beat the heat. We'll walk the trails until midday, have lunch at the lodge, rest for an hour or two—and then head back out. Every time I've been, I've seen wild orangutan, which is very exciting. It's essential that you wear leech socks. These little bloodsuckers are thick on the plants along the trails. But this is good because it means that there are lots of mammals around! After dinner, we often go out on a night tour. You'll take a vehicle with a strong light in the back, manned by one of the local guides. It's amazing what you'll see. On one twelve-mile drive, we saw Bornean Tarsier, Buffy Fish Owl, Colugo, Barred Eagle Owl, Red Giant Flying Squirrel, and Indian Civet. You'll also sometimes see elephants at night. They are smaller than other Asian elephants. Initially it was thought that they were feral, but studies have shown that they're genetically distinct."

One of Susan's fondest memories of Danum Valley involves a Pitta and a client. "I had a lady on one trip, a visual artist, who was suffering from macular degeneration. She said on a number of occasions that she had come because she wanted to see some of Borneo's beautiful birds before her eyesight left. We were out on the trail, and I heard the high-pitched whistle of a Black-and-Crimson Pitta off in the bush. It's very difficult to entice this bird out; to have a chance to see them, you need to head into the thick forest. The five or six of us in the group headed in. I located the bird fairly quickly, sitting a foot off the ground—a stunning creature, with a bright crimson chest, black head, and electric blue back. The woman with the failing eyesight was not able to pick it out. She had her binoculars up as I was trying to explain its location. I could see it was very frustrating to her. I looked to the bird and then looked back to her again. This time, her face radiated; I knew she'd found it. The next time I looked at her, she was crying. She told me that she never thought she would see something so beautiful. Soon after, I had a tear in my eye, too."

SUSAN MEYERS (www.birdingworldwide.com.au) has been studying the fauna of Australia and Asia for over twenty years. She has been a birder and passionate naturalist since early childhood, running around barefoot in the bush chasing birds, lizards, and aquatic insects. After her university studies in biological sciences, Susan moved to Japan where she lived for four years, learning the language and studying the natural history and culture. Once a qualified nursing practitioner, Susan has also worked as a scuba-dive instructor on Australia's Great Barrier Reef in Queensland. She has published papers and articles on ornithology and general ecology in a variety of scientific journals and magazines. She has now traveled to almost every country in Asia and leads tour groups to many destinations in this region. Susan has a deep affection for and appreciation of Asia and its wildlife and she believes that "the combination of incredible and diverse wildlife, ancient and fascinating cultures, and the best food in the world is unique to this amazing continent." Her involvement in nature tourism now exceeds fifteen years. Susan loves to explore new areas and in the little spare time she has, she recently undertook scouting trips to Burma, Palawan, Cambodia, Taiwan, Sumatra, and Halmahera. She has recently begun work on a new field guide to the birds of Borneo. She is a full-time leader with Victor Emanuel Nature Tours.

IF YOU GO

➤ **Getting There:** Visitors access Danum Valley by flying first to the city of Kota Kinabalu, then on to the town of Lahad Datu. From there, it's a two-hour drive (lodge provides transfers). Kota Kinabalu is served by Malaysia Airlines via London, Los Angeles, and Tokyo.

➤ **Best Time to Visit:** Temperatures are very consistent, in the low eighties year-round; the wettest months are November to February.

➤ **Guides:** A number of tour companies lead trips to Borneo, including Victor Emanuel Nature Tours (800-328-8368; www.ventbirds.com), and Wings Birding Tours (888-293-6443; www.wings birds.com). Borneo Rainforest Lodge has guides available.

➤ **Accommodations:** Borneo Rainforest Lodge (888-359-8655; www.borneorainforestlodge.com) is the accommodation of choice for Danum Valley visitors.

AMAZONIA

RECOMMENDED BY **Bret Whitney**

DESTINATION

10

Bret Whitney has spent a good part of the last twenty years leading trips and exploring on his own in some of the remotest sections of the Amazon basin. When I asked him to share a single favorite place, he was hard-pressed to do so; there are simply too many wonderful venues that he feels an attachment to. So we decided to chat about the region in a big-picture sense, with mention of a few of his favorite lodges.

"The Amazon basin holds far and away more species of birds per square mile than any other place on Earth!" Bret effused. "There are numerous sites that boast in excess of 500 species in a radius of six miles. I can go on and on with these sorts of gee-whiz statistics . . ."

Amazonia—the region defined by the watersheds of the Amazon basin—is a sprawling area, nearly the size of the lower forty-eight in the United States. Bordered by the Andes to the west, it spreads east across much of the top half of South America, encompassing parts of Colombia, Ecuador, Peru, Bolivia, and much of Brazil. Amazonia is home to well over 1,000 bird species; new species are discovered most years, and ornithologists are quite certain that additional undiscovered species are flitting about the forest canopy as this book goes to press. "The Amazon River, together with some of her mighty tributaries, separate many species of birds that never fly across," Bret continued. "This creates a series of vast blocks of isolated species. This, and the phenomenon of 'species-packing' (the capacity for related species to maintain their separate identities even when inhabiting the same place), are the principal forces that have produced the overwhelmingly rich avifauna of the Amazon basin."

The number of microhabitats across Amazonia are dizzying, but Bret Whitney is one person who can interpret them for the less informed. "From a birding perspective, there are two major forest divisions: terra firma (never flooded) versus seasonally flooded forest. Within each of these two major biomes one can identify several additional habitats of more restricted and patchy distribution defined mostly by soil characteristics. Prominent among these are 'blackwater' habitats (soils very sandy and nutrient-poor, rivers consequently steeped in acidic tannins imparting a 'Coca-Cola' color to the water); and 'whitewater/clearwater' habitats (soils on richer loams and clays supporting much higher diversity of plants, so called because the rivers carry heavy loads of silt eroded from their Andean headwaters). Each supports distinctive species assemblages. The seasonally flooded forest components of the blackwater system are called igapó (almost always flooded, very low plant diversity) and chavascal (a very narrow band of low-lying, seasonally flooded forest). For whitewater systems, seasonally flooded forest may be separated into várzea (with high plant diversity on nutrient-rich soils renewed with Andean sediments every year during the flooding cycle) and 'whitewater river islands,' which migrate along the courses of the major rivers and hold a suite of 'specialty' birds not found in nearby várzea forest. Many 'microhabitats' in Amazonia further complement the species richness, such as scattered scrubby zones on sandy soils called campiñas (Brazil) or varillales (Peru), bamboo tracts, Heliconia thickets, vine tangles, etc."

The experience of birding in Amazonia is overwhelmingly exciting. "On clear mornings, the forest begins to awaken with a chorus of bird sounds just as it gets light enough to see your way to the breakfast table," Bret continued. "You know that there are at least 400 species of birds within about one mile of where you sit. That in itself inspires you to wolf down your coffee, eggs, and toast in anticipation of . . . well, that's just it . . . there is no telling what wonderful things lie ahead! These forests are so rich that every day brings new discoveries, and presents new puzzles and questions, challenging one's senses to the max to learn to find and identify the many exciting birds that are regular members of mixed-species flocks you might come upon. There are the secretive antbirds that obtain virtually all of their food by capturing insects and spiders fleeing from voracious swarms of army ants; or the special birds that live only on river islands just a hundred yards from where you stand on the bank. Bird diversity is so great that every day is quite different, even on the very same trails.

"The variety of sounds is also fabulous, ranging from spritely chirrs in the undergrowth to loud yelps and caws high in the canopy. A productive early morning atop a canopy tower in Amazonia can rank among the most memorable events of a birder's life! It is not unusual to see and hear nearly 100 species in just two to three hours; identifying a high proportion of the ones parading by at eye level and below in your and neighboring trees is the fun of it. Many canopy birds are rarely, if ever, seen well from the ground. Nighttime excursions also raise goosebumps, as owls, nightjars, and pootoos sing to the full moon and stare eerily into spotlights. Birding in

Amazonia invariably results in encounters with an amazing variety of other wild creatures, which greatly enriches an already wonderful experience."

Bret Whitney has spent enough time in the Amazon basin to be able to go it on his own. But staying at a lodge is still a pleasant experience for him—and a must for birders who haven't logged much time in the jungle. "There are a number of modern, comfortable birding lodges in Amazonia that display a combination of characteristics that make them especially rewarding for the visiting birder," Bret added. "Essentials when selecting a lodge include access by hiking trail or boat to as many of the habitats and microhabitats as possible; the presence of at least one tower at canopy level or higher (as that's where much of the action is); and availability of English-speaking local guides with good knowledge of the birds and birding areas. [A list of lodges appears below.]

BRET WHITNEY grew up birding in the Midwest, mostly in Indiana, where he graduated from Earlham College. He is well known for his ability to identify birds by their calls and songs, which has led to his discovery in South America and Madagascar of multiple species new to science. Bret is one of the founders of Field Guides (www.fieldguides.com), a Research Associate of the Museum of Natural Science at Louisiana State University, an Associate of the Laboratory of Ornithology at Cornell and recipient of the American Birding Association's prestigious "Ludlow Griscom" award for his research on Amazonian birdlife. Bret guides most of Field Guides' Brazil tours and, with Brazilian colleagues, he is coauthoring a series of regional field guides to the birds of Brazil.

IF YOU GO

► **Getting There:** Alta Floresta, Brazil, is served from Cuiabá on TRIP Airlines, which is served from São Paulo or Rio de Janeiro on Varig and TAM Airlines. Iquitos, Peru, is served from Lima by Aero Condor, Lan Peru, Star Peru, and Wayra Peru. Cuzco, Peru (near Madre de Dios) is served by Aero Condor, Star Peru, and Lan Peru.

► **Best Time to Visit:** Amazonia's rich bird life is present year-round, though the period from June to October has the coolest temperatures, and driest conditions.

► **Guides:** The lodges below have resident guides. Many embarking on a trip here will retain a tour company to lead them to multiple spots. Bret leads trips for Field Guides (800-728-4953;

www.fieldguides.com), but also recommends Victor Emanuel Nature Tours (800-328-8368; www.ventbirds.com) and Birding Brazil (+55 92-638-4540; www.birdingbraziltours.com).

➤ **Accommodations:** A few of the lodges that meet Bret's high standards include: Cristalino Jungle Lodge in Alta Floresta, Brazil (+55 66-3512-7100; www.cristalinolodge.com.br); Explorama Lodges around Iquitos, Peru (800-707-5275; www.explorama.com); Amazonia Lodge in Madre de Dios, Peru (+51 8423-6159; www.ecoamazonia.com); Manu Wildlife Center, Madre de Dios, Peru (+51 8425-5255; www.manu-wildlife-center.com); and Tambopata Research Center in Madre de Dios, Peru, which is operated by Rainforest Expeditions (www.perunature.com) [NOTE: Tambopata lacks canopy walk]. Amazonia Expedition LTDA (amex@argo.com.br) provides live-aboard luxury on river boats that can access undisturbed habitats beyond reach any other way.

MONTEREY BAY NATIONAL MARINE SANCTUARY

RECOMMENDED BY **Debra Love Shearwater**

The Monterey Bay area has seductive attractions for many. For golfers, it's the great links of Carmel—Pebble Beach, Spyglass, and for the lucky few, Cypress Point. For marine life enthusiasts, it's the world-class Monterey Aquarium. For fans of John Steinbeck, it's the muse of Cannery Row. And for birders—especially those interested in seabirds—it's the waters of the Monterey Bay National Marine Sanctuary (MBNMS).

"The MBNMS is a world-class place," said Debi Shearwater. "It's the largest federally protected area in the lower forty-eight, even bigger than Yellowstone. The submarine Monterey Bay Canyon is deeper than the Grand Canyon (at 10,663 feet). If you were to talk to marine biologists, they would tell you that the sanctuary is among the five most productive marine ecosystems in the world. If you were to make a list of the marine life in this one place, it's overwhelming—a Serengeti unto itself. I can't think of any place that makes me feel more at home. I never know what to expect, and I'm always excited."

The Monterey Bay National Marine Sanctuary extends far beyond the borders of the bay itself. To the north, it reaches Rocky Point, seven miles north of the Golden Gate Bridge; to the south, it extends to the town of Cambria, in San Luis Obispo County. That's a total shoreline length of 276 miles. The sanctuary stretches an average of thirty miles off-shore, encompassing a total of 5,322 square miles. Within its waters are thirty-three species of marine mammals (including blue, humpback, and gray whales and closer to shore in the kelp forests, ever-beguiling sea otters), 345 species of fish (with great white sharks at the top of the piscine food chain), and ninety-four species of seabirds. "There's so much beauty along the shoreline and so many natural attractions, very few people venture out onto the ocean to see the wildlife there," Debi continued. "As a result, the MBNMS is a vastly underutilized resource."

Which may be all the better for those who do venture out, as the likelihood of encountering

OPPOSITE:
A Sooty Shearwater, one of many shearwater species encountered out on the Monterey Bay National Marine Sanctuary.

crowds is next to nil. (One reason there may be fewer birders on the water is that there's some excellent birding to be had along the shoreline between the Monterey Peninsula and Santa Cruz—some 400 species are recorded each year! However, to see the true seabirds—albatrosses, shearwaters, storm petrels, skuas, jaegers, puffins, murres, and others—one needs to venture beyond the coast by boat.)

"I'll never forget my first visit to Monterey," Debi reminisced. "I came to California in 1976 with my then-husband, via Texas, where I'd first got the birding bug. The first thing I wanted to do was go down to the bay and see those shearwaters (I hadn't changed my surname at that point). I had read a book by Ron Lockley about banding Manx Shearwaters in England, and it fascinated me. When I got down to the the harbor it was covered with Northern Fulmars. It was instant magic—I couldn't believe it, and I've never seen such a thing since.

"When I decided to change my last name, I wanted one that was easy to pronounce and easy to spell. Shearwater—a bird I was fascinated with—seemed like the obvious choice. Later, I traced my family tree. It turns out the Swedish side of my family had always been involved with the sea. And my maiden name was Millichap, and the Millichaps came from the Isle of Man . . . the island that's the namesake for the Manx Shearwater. It all connected."

With an area as vast as the MBNMS, how does one figure out where to go to find bird life? "At the beginning of a given day, I honestly don't know where we're going to go," Debi said. "I look at what's happening with the weather, and combine that with my knowledge of what's been going on out on the water the last few months, and historically at that time of year. My best barometer of the weather is a particular flag near the town of Monterey. On a fall (August through October) day, we might see a variety of shearwaters and storm petrels (including some of the largest concentrations of Ashy Storm-Petrels in the world), Black-footed Albatross, Tufted Puffin, South Polar Skuas, Jaegers, Rhinosceros- and Cassin's Auklets—and perhaps a megararity like a Streaked Shearwater or Red-tailed Tropicbird."

The variety and vitality of the MBNMS keep naturalists like Debi Shearwater always coming back for more. "I was on the water last Friday, and we had a female humpback whale rubbing itself on the bow of the boat; she was using her tail stock and pectoral flippers to hold herself on the boat. She was there for forty minutes; left with two other humpbacks, and then came back again and did it two more times. A little later that day, we saw a great white shark come up and take a sea lion on the surface. All this was less than an hour's run from shore. A week before, we saw eight species of shearwaters in one day—Streaked Shearwater, Greater Shearwater, Manx Shearwater, Flesh-footed Shearwater, Buller's Shearwater, Pink-footed Shearwater, Sooty

Shearwater, and Black-vented Shearwater. It's a world record. As if that weren't enough, a Brown Booby flew over our heads!

"Many people know little about seabird conservation," Debi added. "But a few come out to the coast, step onto a boat, and see what there is to offer out there. No matter what we see at the top, I try to stress to people that there's even more going on under the surface of the sea."

DEBRA LOVE SHEARWATER is founder of Shearwater Journeys (www.shearwaterjourneys. com), a name synonymous with seabirding trips from Monterey, California. Over 50,000 birders from all over the world have joined her on boat trips since 1976. A full-time marine naturalist-birder, she has logged more than 1800 days at sea, visiting countless places, from the Bering Sea to Antarctica. Enthusiastic about all marine life, Debi has worked as a research assistant on pro-grams focusing on blue whales, several species of dolphins, and leatherback sea turtles. For the past several years, she has been leading expedition trips to remote areas of the world, including Antarctica, Iceland, Spitsbergen, New Zealand's sub-Antarctic Islands, and the Russian Far East. Featured in numerous books and television programs, Debi has coproduced her own DVD— *Through the Seasons: An Introduction to the Seabirds and Marine Mammals of Monterey Bay*. Debi is a past member of the board of directors of the American Birding Association.

IF YOU GO

▶ **Getting There:** Monterey is about a two hours' drive from the San Jose airport, which is served by most major airlines.

▶ **Best Time to Visit:** There's activity year-round on Monterey Bay; Debi Shearwater leads a majority of her trips from August to October.

▶ **Guides:** Debi Shearwater leads many tours on Monterey Bay through Shearwater Journeys (831-637-8527; www.shearwaterjourneys.com). Monterey Seabirds (831-375-4658; www.monterey seabirds.com) also leads tours.

▶ **Accommodations:** Monterey and the surrounding region are popular vacation destinations, and offer a wide range of accommodations. Contact the Monterey County Convention and Visitors Bureau (888-221-1010; www.montereyinfo.org) or the Pacific Grove Chamber of Commerce (800-656-6650; www.pacificgrove.org) for more information.

POINT REYES NATIONAL SEASHORE

RECOMMENDED BY **Phil Eager**

Each you time you drive north over the Golden Gate Bridge and look out on the stark beauty of the Marin Headlands, you can thank the farsightedness of Marin's leading citizens that those hills are not festooned with McMansions. About thirty-five miles farther north in Marin County, there's an equally inspired example of preservation at work: Point Reyes National Seashore.

"If you were new to West Coast birding, Point Reyes would be a great place to start," said Phil Eager, who moved to San Francisco from the East Coast a few years back. "My wife and I joke that one of the reasons we pushed for relocation was that we'd see a whole new set of birds. Point Reyes gives you a great snapshot of what's around. In many respects, it reminds me of Cape May—there's riparian woodland, salt and freshwater marshes, beaches—everything. It's a pretty tough combination to beat. You can spend a day looking at fairly common birds, or chasing specialty species. It's one of those great generalist places; you can do pretty much whatever you want to do, depending on your expertise or energy level."

The panoply of birding opportunities Point Reyes offers is in part the result of the tremendous variety of habitats assembled in this 111-square-mile park, which lies on a peninsula separated from the mainland by the eastern San Andreas Fault. From beaches and cliffsides to estuaries, ponds, pasture land with working ranches and forest, it's all here. The plentitude Point Reyes offers also results from its ideal location on north-south and east-west flyways. Given the abundance of protected habitat and the great potential for vagrants (especially when one considers that the peninsula juts ten miles west into the Pacific), it's not surprising that birders have recorded nearly 500 species at Point Reyes! The preserve is crisscrossed with hiking trails, and roads lead to the far points of the park, including Point Reyes Lighthouse, which rests on the park's westernmost point. Here, pelagic species like Brandt's Cormorants, Pigeon Guillemots, and Surf Scoters can often be seen; Tufted Puffin are occasional visitors here, too. The lighthouse,

OPPOSITE:
California Quail are commonly found around Point Reyes.

61

DESTINATION

12

which dates back to 1870, helped mariners steer clear of these headlands until 1975, when it was replaced by an automated light. Having endured several earthquakes and some of the windiest weather California can muster, it's now maintained as a museum.

Point Reyes's status as a birding hub is underscored by the presence and influence of the Point Reyes Bird Observatory. Established in 1965 (three years after the park was established), PRBO Conservation Science (as it's now known) conducts extensive research throughout the park—and throughout the American West and beyond—to gauge the well-being of ecosystems and protect and enhance biodiversity. Though PRBO recently moved its headquarters from just south of the park (in Stinson Beach) to nearby Petaluma, they still maintain the Palomarin Field Station, where visitors can see demonstrations of mist-netting and learn more about PRBO's current projects.

There's pretty much always something to see at Point Reyes. "There are lots of different tacks you can take if you have a day to spend at Point Reyes," Phil continued. "We'll decide what to do depending on what we're after or what strikes our fancy on any given day—we have a basic circuit, but we can easily detour. In the fall, for example, we'll probably head out toward the lighthouse. Along the way, there are active and inactive ranches. The land grants go back to the 1850s; even though it's a national park, you have some private in-holdings. There are some eucalyptus and cypress trees that were planted as windbreaks. On a good day—that is, a windy and overcast day—you might be able to spend a whole day there seeing what's hiding out in the trees, which can include stray warblers and other songbirds not normally seen on the West Coast. If there's not much happening in the trees, we'll continue out to the lighthouse or toward Chimney Rock for seabirds. The fall can also be a great time for the one-mile hike to Abbott's Lagoon which, when the water levels are right, can host a good variety of shorebirds (including the occasional rarity). Other times, we'll start with the creeks in the woodlands right near the main visitor center in Bear Valley. There are some good trails there to look for warblers and kinglets, and in the winter it can be a great spot for Varied Thrushes and sparrows. The winter in general is a good time for wintering ducks and raptors throughout Point Reyes. Out along Limantour Road, there's more good riparian habitat that has a slightly different mix of birds than the other spots, including a nice population of Wrentits. Olema Marsh is a great morning spot. You'll find Cinnamon Teal and calling Sora and Virginia Rails on the water and in the marsh. There are dead trees with hawks and woodpeckers. Olema is also a great photography spot; there's a ridge in the background, and in the morning there's mist burning off the marsh.

"One of the best reasons to visit," Phil added, "is that Point Reyes is drop-dead gorgeous. Birders can sometimes get a bad reputation for going to less beautiful places to see certain birds; even on a bad birding day, Point Reyes is a beautiful place to visit. And, if all else fails, you can always hike to places like Arch Rock or along the Tomales Point Trail where Tule Elk can be seen."

Come December, even generally sunny Marin County cannot escape the cool rains that come to the northern California coast. But a little inclement weather cannot dull the spirits of Point Reyes's annual Christmas bird count. "It is consistently up there in the top-five for Christmas counts, both in terms of birds and counters," Phil continued. "At Point Reyes, it's as much a social activity as a scientific study. The Point Reyes count 'circle' (a standard geographic size set by National Audubon Society for all of the Christmas Bird Counts) is divided into smaller regions by geographic areas; my group (led by the incomparable Rich Stallcup, one of the founders of PRBO) focuses on wintering birds in Olema Marsh and the surrounding areas. There's a good-natured spirit of competition as people scour the park; people are always trying to one-up each other.

"At the end of the day, everyone meets at the Dance Palace in the little hamlet of Point Reyes Station. The birders rent it out for a dinner. As we're eating, each area calls out the birds they've found. It's a badge of honor to find something unexpected or new. Sometimes the count will have a list of over 200 species."

When conditions are right, the birders of Point Reyes will gather to witness a somewhat macabre spectacle. "One of the birds people go to Point Reyes to see is the Black Rail, which is fairly rare in the Bay Area and even harder to actually see. There's a spot near the southern end of Tomales Bay where, if there's a high tide on a winter weekend, you'll see a number of birders. On one occasion, I showed up and there were at least thirty-five people lined up on top of the dike, with Lord-knows-how-many hundreds of thousands of dollars' worth of optics, waiting for the Black Rails to pop out of the reeds as the tide flows in. We're not the only ones there waiting for the rails; as the tide moves in, there is a host of Great Blue Herons and Great Egrets moving around. Invariably, the Black Rails begin popping out; eight times out of ten, they get devoured. It was a surreal feeling, knowing what's going to happen, but looking on nonetheless. I do wonder how many birders have seen their 'lifer' Black Rail here only seconds before it's consumed by a heron or egret."

PHIL EAGER is senior associate general counsel at the Sierra Club (www.sierraclub.org). Before joining the Sierra Club, he was a corporate lawyer for eleven years. Phil's passion for birding began at Cape May, New York's Central Park, and Jamaica Bay National Wildlife Refuge. His birding adventures have taken him and his wife to southeastern Arizona, Alaska, the Salton Sea in southern California, the Dry Tortugas, Hawaii, and the Lower Rio Grande Valley in Texas. A native of Connecticut, Phil is a graduate of the University of Pennsylvania and the University of Pennsylvania Law School.

IF YOU GO

➤ **Getting There:** Point Reyes is roughly an hour north of San Francisco . . . depending on traffic on the Golden Gate Bridge.

➤ **Best Time to Visit:** Point Reyes has something to offer birders year-round. Winter is best for ducks and raptors, spring for migrants.

➤ **Guides:** PRBO Palomarin Field Station Visitor Center (www.prbo.org) has many resources for self-guided tours. The California Naturalist (www.calnaturalist.com) offers personalized tours.

➤ **Accommodations:** There are a number of pleasant inns around Point Reyes that accommodate birders. For a list, contact Pt. Reyes Lodging (800-539-1872; www.ptreyes.com).

SACRAMENTO VALLEY

RECOMMENDED BY **Steven J. McCormick**

Motorists speeding along Interstate 5 between Sacramento and Red Bluff, California, are struck, if anything, by the blandness of their immediate surroundings. Fields of rice and other grains unfold on either side of the highway, stretching to the Coast Range in the west and the Sierra Nevadas in the east. This landscape is punctuated by the occasional grain silo or truck stop. Though uninspiring at a glance, just a few miles off the highway (and in some places, just a few hundred yards off the road) rests a vibrant haven of avian life in the remnants of one of North America's great wetlands—the Sacramento Valley.

"As a boy, I was torn between growing up to be a baseball player or a forest ranger," Steve McCormick began. "The trees won out. My curiosity about trees evolved into an interest in field botany, and I began spending time at Point Reyes. The many birders I encountered there were interested in learning more about plants, and I wanted to learn more about birds. My original draw to the Sacramento Valley was hunting, but soon I realized that there in my backyard was some of the world's greatest birding."

The Sacramento Valley is one of the bread baskets of America. The wetlands that once spread across the valley have largely been drained to make way for fields, the rivers and creeks tamed to prevent the flooding that once sustained this habitat. While 90 percent of the central valley's wetlands and grasslands are gone, the Pacific Flyway remains. Each year, an abundance of waterfowl—three million ducks and upward of 750,000 geese—migrate to the valley from as far away as Siberia, wintering in the swatches of habitat that are still intact. Visitors include Pintails; Mallards; Widgeon; Northern Shoveler; and Snow, Ross's, and White-fronted Geese. (Indeed, the valley is the most important waterfowl wintering area along the Pacific Flyway.) The core of this habitat is contained in the Sacramento National Wildlife Refuge Complex. The complex—which consists of the Sacramento, Delevan, Colusa, Sutter, Butte Sink, and Sacramento River Refuges—is described as

"an oasis in a sea of agriculture." The first five refuges comprise nearly 25,000 acres of grassland, marshes, ponds, and seasonal wetlands. The Sacramento River National Wildlife Refuge protects invaluable riparian habitat along seventy-seven miles of the river. This refuge and the other preserves in the valley are intensively managed to maintain critical waterfowl wintering habitat.

"I feel a visceral draw to the valley," Steve continued. "Though it's been significantly converted to agriculture, the natural habitat that remains is quite special. There are still some grasslands left with vernal pools. The Valley Oak riparian habitat is unique to California, yet so dense and lush that it's very un-California."

The Sacramento Valley is not just for waterfowl. The riparian forests are also the home of many songbirds—Bullock's Orioles, Ash-throated Flycatchers, and Black-headed Grosbeaks, to name a few. While many songbird species are in decline in North America, the songbirds native to the Sacramento River region are rebounding. Studies show that Bullock's Oriole populations have increased by over 10 percent, and that Spotted Towhee populations have increased by a whopping 26 percent over the course of a fifteen-year habitat restoration effort. Overseen by PRBO Conservation Science and conducted by a patchwork of government agencies and environmental groups, the restoration has focused on returning farmland to its earlier riparian forest state.

"In the late seventies when the first work was being done to restore the habitat along the river, there were just little patches left," Steve said. "The trajectory was heading toward collapse—or at least an extremely dysfunctional system. One of the breakthroughs came when we realized that acquiring some spots along the river for habitat wouldn't do it—we had to think about the dynamics of the larger system. We felt it necessary to reproduce the original flooding along the river. Tens of thousands of trees were planted; more important, we aggressively acquired land and opened the levees. With the help of PRBO, we designed an active reserve system and developed flow patterns. There's no question that the program has been successful. One of the birds that had been virtually eliminated is the Yellow-billed Cuckoo. I've seen them now in the restored habitat. Having been a small part of that conservation work is very satisfying."

Steve is a waterfowl hunter as well as a birder, and there is less of a contradiction here than some might think. "Any experienced duck hunter is an incredibly good bird watcher, almost by definition," Steve continued. "Every duck hunter I know is very good at spotting; you learn early on how to identify the different species of ducks and sex them. This draws your attention to other birds. Sitting in a duck blind in a Tule marsh watching Snow Geese, Ross's Geese, tons of Pintail and Wood Ducks is one of the most relaxing things I can imagine.

13

DESTINATION

OPPOSITE:
A brilliant sunset
provides a backdrop
for the Sacramento
National Wildlife
Refuge.

"This past fall, I was on a duck-hunting trip in the valley. My party arrived in the afternoon—five or six duck hunters in all. We could easily have gone hunting, but instead we went birding at a little Audubon refuge near the town of Willows. We got there about 3:30. On cue, birds came rising off a restored natural marsh; my guess is that they were moving into rice fields to feed that night. At first all the Mallards came off, then the Wigeons, then Green-winged Teal. It's always surprising how they separate themselves out. There must have been a hundred thousand birds in the sweep of our view. It was an incredible scene—looking across the flooded Tule marsh, with a line of willows and oaks and cottonwoods at the marsh's edge, and the sun just setting behind the hills to the west, illuminating a thin layer of clouds and a tiny sliver of crescent moon. Film simply couldn't capture the moment, the smell of the loamy, fecund earth, the sounds of the swarming birds. It's such a sensual experience, made all that much better by being there with good friends who share the same feelings."

STEVEN J. McCORMICK is president and chief executive officer of the Nature Conservancy (www.nature.org), the world's largest environmental organization, with operations in all fifty states and more than thirty countries. He has led the organization since 2001. Steve joined TNC shortly after graduating from the University of California, Hastings College of Law, in 1976. He sits on several boards, including the Sustainable Forestry Board, Harvard Dialogue Group Advisory Panel, and the Advisory Board of the U.C. Berkeley College of Natural Resources.

IF YOU GO

➤ **Getting There:** The closest major airport to the Sacramento Valley is the Sacramento International Airport, which is served by most major carriers. From here, prime birding locations begin within an hour's drive north.

➤ **Best Time to Visit:** While interesting avian life is present year-round, November and December are considered the best months for viewing wintering waterfowl.

➤ **Guides:** The Sacramento Valley National Wildlife Refuge Complex website (www.fws.gov/sacramentovalleyrefuges/index.htm) has excellent resources for do-it-yourself birding.

➤ **Accommodations:** The town of Willows, California, is a good base of operations for birding the Sacramento Valley, and offers modest chain-variety accommodations.

SAN GERARDO DE DOTA

RECOMMENDED BY **Ralph Paonessa**

Ralph Paonessa initially came to San Gerardo de Dota in search of hummingbirds. He's been returning again and again to witness the majesty of the Resplendent Quetzal.

"When I first went to Costa Rica, I was hoping to visit as many places as I could to see hummingbirds, as they are of special interest to me," Ralph said. "Hummingbirds tend to be higher-altitude birds, and you generally find different species at different elevations. Of course, in Costa Rica, you can go from sea level to 12,000 feet, so there's great variety. I was at one lodge that was at around 3,000 feet and saw what hummers I could, then visited another spot at roughly 5,000 feet and did the same. Someone told me that I'd find a number of hummingbirds that I wouldn't find at many other places at the Savegre River area near San Gerardo de Dota, which is at about 7,000 feet in the cloud forests of the Talamanca Mountains.

"It was quite an adventure to get there. You take the Interamerican Highway from San Jose, climbing to 10,000 feet as you go through the pass at Cerro de La Muerte. Considering the road's narrowness and the citizenry's tendency to pass at will (despite the lack of any passing lane), you'd think it was named for the dangerous driving, though in fact it's named for the many people who tried to cross the mountains from the jungles far below and perished due to the elements. I made it safely, and found at least ten different species of hummingbirds. At the lodge where I was staying, people encouraged me to go find a Resplendent Quetzal. They said I'd be blown away by their beauty. (I learned later that Resplendent Quetzals and hummingbirds are actually distant relatives.)"

Costa Rica is much celebrated in ecotourism circles for its natural beauty, access to both the Caribbean and the Pacific, and its abundance of habitat—from tropical rain forest to montane. For new listers, Costa Rica is must-visit venue; with some professional guidance, less-seasoned birders can boost their neotropic numbers significantly, while adding such endemics as Black

Guan, Sulphur-winged Parakeet, Fiery-throated Hummingbird, Lattice-tailed Trogon, and Long-tailed Silky-flycatcher. Though not endemic—and not even excessively difficult to find—a bird that hard-core listers and casual naturalists alike will step out of their way to see is the Resplendent Quetzal. Roger Tory Peterson, who called the male Resplendent Quetzal the most spectacular bird in the New World, described it in the Field Guide to the Birds of Mexico as an "intense emerald and golden green with red belly and white undertail . . . the body measures about fifteen inches but the tail, rich in iridescent blues and greens above and subtle white below, can extend as much as thirty inches." The tail feathers referenced here are actually streamer feathers that spring from the bird's shoulders. "The further they are along in their breeding plumage, the longer the streamers," Ralph explained. "Considering how colorful these birds are, you'd think they'd stand out like a sore thumb. Yet they're not that easy to spot. It certainly helps to find a guide."

The Resplendent Quetzal has a significant place among the cultures of Mesoamerica. The Maya believed that the bird was sacred, and their kings wore headdresses festooned with Quetzal feathers; the Aztec ruler Montezuma is said to have worn a cloak adorned with seven hundred Quetzal plumes. One of the most common motifs in Mesoamerican art is the Quetzalcoatl, or "feathered snake" (Quetzal meaning "long green feather" and coatl meaning "snake"). The Quetzalcoatl plays different roles in different religious traditions, alternately being the creator, god of the wind, god of water, and fertility god.

Ralph encountered his first Quetzal through a string of newfound European friends. "At the lodge, I befriended an amateur photographer from Switzerland named Thomas who had met a German photographer who was staying at another lodge. The German had told Thomas that the owner of his lodge knew the location of a Resplendent Quetzal nest, and was going to lead him to see it. We made plans to accompany him. The lodge owner was brimming with energy and was constantly in motion. But he knew where the birds were. We followed him through the woods, across meadows with horses grazing, then across a narrow log bridge over the raging Rio Savegre. I was carrying about $10,000 worth of camera gear and had second thoughts, but kept going. We got to the spot, and the male Quetzal flew in. I wasn't able to photograph the male on this occasion, but I returned two more times. On the last trip, the male flew in and perched nicely. One of the shots of that bird is blown up on the wall of my office."

The end product of bird photography—be it a print on the wall or the cover of a glossy calendar—is one of the vocation's pleasures. Ralph explained another. "One of the real joys of photographing birds is that you spend quite a bit of time with just a few birds, and you end up

DESTINATION

14

OPPOSITE:
No less an authority
than Roger Tory
Peterson called the
Resplendent Quetzal
the most spectacular
bird in the New
World.

seeing behaviors and activities that most birders, who have less time to spend, might miss. I get a privileged view of these lovely little animals. It doesn't matter whether you're photographing a Resplendent Quetzal or a House Sparrow. You try to spend days with your subject, as it takes as long to get good photographs of a common bird as it does for a rare bird.

"Bird photography is also a great motivation for travel," Ralph added. "If you want to photograph a Resplendent Quetzal or Wandering Albatross, you have to go where they live!"

RALPH PAONESSA has been leading bird photography teaching trips to his favorite birding places around the world since 1997 through his company, Ralph Paonessa Photography Workshops (www.rpphotos.com). His photos have appeared in magazines such as *Outdoor Photographer*, *WildBird* (including several covers), *Birder's World*, *Birdwatcher's Digest*, *Nature and Wildlife*, *Martha Stewart Living*, and *Outdoor Traveler*. Ralph's work has also been featured in calendars by Audubon, Barnes and Noble, *Birder's World*, Sierra Club, World Wildlife Fund, At-A-Glance, Pet Prints, and the Himalayan Calendar, and in numerous books, including *Focus on the Wild* (published by the Texas Valley Land Fund). Ralph is based in Ridgecrest, California, in the heart of the Mojave Desert.

IF YOU GO

► **Getting There:** San Gerardo de Dota is roughly three hours by car from San Jose, Costa Rica, which is served by many carriers, including American, Continental, and Delta Airlines. (Less intrepid drivers may wish to travel during the day.)

► **Best Time to Visit:** Resplendent Quetzals are present year-round.

► **Guides:** Most leading birding tour companies lead adventures to Costa Rica, though many do not visit San Gerardo de Dota. The lodges below all have access to local birding guides.

► **Accommodations:** Several area lodges cater to birders, including Savegre Hotel (506-771-9686; www.savegrehotel.com), Savegre Mountain Hotel (506-740-1028; www.savegre.co.cr) and Trogon Lodge (506-293-8181; www.grupomawamba.com).

PODOCARPUS NATIONAL PARK

RECOMMENDED BY **Rose Ann Rowlett**

Rose Ann Rowlett paid Podocarpus National Park about as high a praise as any serious birder could muster: "I've been going to Podocarpus since 1988 at least once a year," she began, "and I can still get lifers there. The forest gives up its secrets slowly, and it may take a lifetime to find them all and see them well. If you look at other things like plants and butterflies, it takes more than one lifetime. I love traveling to different continents—some of the richest places in the world—though I have to say, I'd be happy if I only got to bird in Ecuador and Peru. There's scarce wildlife in these places that can be seen with patience and effort, and it's a joy to behold."

Podocarpus National Park is located in the southern Andes of Ecuador, near the towns of Loja in the west and Zamora in the east. Named for the Podocarpus tree (the only native Ecuadorian conifer), the park preserves 1,000 square miles of territory that includes virgin forest, mountains reaching almost 12,000 feet, more than a hundred glacial lakes, and countless streams. Much of the terrain consists of páramo—a form of high-altitude grassland. "The range of habitat you find in Podocarpus gives you an incredible sampling of east-slope Andean birds," Rose Ann continued. "There's also fascinating mammal life. The Podocarpus tree makes lovely furniture, and stocks have been tremendously depleted where they can be accessed by roads. Fortunately, the park has many riverine canyons where foresters couldn't get across." Over 500 bird species have been identified in Podocarpus to date; some believe the species count could reach 800.

There are two primary access points to the wonders of Podocarpus. The first is the main entrance at Cajanuma, a habitat of cloud forest and elfin forest/páramo at the north end of the park, which some hail as the finest single birding spot in the world. "This is the high-elevation

(zona alta) entrance," Rose Ann continued. "There's a fabulous road that takes you through temperate forest to the ranger station. A variety of trails lead from there. You're at 10,000-foot elevation, and you can go up or down from this point." The forests surrounding Cajanuma are home to a startling list of avifauna, including over sixty species of hummingbirds, eighty species of tanagers, Bearded Guan, Rainbow Starfrontlet, Chestnut-bellied Cotinga, and the White-breasted Parakeet. "It was believed that the White-breasted Parakeet was endemic to the region," Rose Ann added, "though recently an expedition from Louisiana State University found them in northern Peru."

The other popular entrance to Podocarpus is on the east slope of the mountains, at Río Bombuscaro. "This is the lower-elevation (zona baja) entrance," Rose Ann continued. "There's a fabulous trail that goes along and above the rushing Bombuscaro River. It leads to a clearing where there's a rangers' headquarters. The trails go for a long way in this lovely wilderness, and it's also incredibly rich in bird life, which includes big mixed flocks of tanagers, Olive Finch, White-tipped Sicklebill, Black-streaked Puffbird, Chestnut-tipped Toucanet, Ecuadorian Tyrannulet, and Amazonian Cock-of-the-Rock. Ten minutes up the road from the entrance, there's a small lodge called Copalinga—a little bed-and-breakfast with beautiful bungalows scattered above the river. There are lots of birds on the property, and the owner is a wonderful cook."

One of the most recent additions to the list of Podocarpus species—and for that matter, species of the world—is the Jocotoco Antpitta. The bird has been described by the World Land Trust as having "a round body usually the size and shape of a grapefruit, and legs which they use like pogo sticks to hop across the forest floor." A member of the antbird family, the first Jocotoco Antpitta was discovered by ornithologist Robert Ridgely in 1997 in what is now the Cerro Tapichalaca Reserve just south of Podacarpus, and bears his name—Grallaria ridgelyi.

It was at Cajanuma that Rose Ann had one of her richest Podocarpus experiences. "I used to lead tours in the Cajanuma region with my brother," she said. "On one occasion, we had fourteen people. I took seven people up to the páramo; John took the other half of the group on a circular trail toward the entrance road. In the course of the morning, my group came upon a fantastic sight—an Andean Pygmy Owl being mobbed by a Sword-billed Hummingbird. Thinking it couldn't get much better than that, we then sighted an Undulated Antpitta. As we were coming down to our tour bus, our driver was waiting, in an excited state. 'Venga, venga!' he said. He shepherded us onto the bus, and roared down the road. Soon, we reached my brother and his group. They were watching a Spectacled Bear (the only surviving species of bear native to South America). The bear had crawled up into a tree and had been eating fruit. John's group looked on as the bear had taken a nap on one of the limbs of the tree. It was waking up as we arrived. The bear ate a bit

DESTINATION

15

OPPOSITE:
A Violet-tailed
Sylph, one of sixty
species of humming-
birds found in the
higher elevations of
Podocarpus
National Park.

75

more fruit and then crawled down the trunk of the tree and disappeared into the forest.

"Each time I've been there with a group since, I point out the spot. A few years back I was trying to break in Jay VanderGaast, who was going to begin leading trips in Podocarpus for Field Guides. As we came to the pull-off where I'd seen the bear, I was telling him about that morning. Jay pointed into the trees and asked 'What's that thing?' It was another Spectacled Bear in the forest canopy, in the exact same spot where we'd seen the bear before!"

ROSE ANN ROWLETT has been birding since her second-grade teacher influenced her and her brother to start identifying Texas migrants using Richard Pough's eastern Audubon guide with the marvelous Eckelberry illustrations. She developed an enduring love for neotropical birds beginning in 1960, when mentor Edgar Kincaid took Rose Ann, her brother, John, and their friend Frank Oatman on the first of many school-holiday birding trips to Mexico. Trained as a biologist with a specialty in ornithology, Rose Ann combines a broad natural-history background with special interests in bird song and behavior. She began guiding tours in 1975 and was one of the founders of Field Guides in 1985. Over the years she has guided more than 250 birding tours, specializing in trips to South America (her favorite continent) but detouring regularly to Africa, Madagascar, and Australasia. More recent forays to Malaysia, Thailand, and Bhutan have generated new enthusiasm for pheasants, pittas, babblers, and broadbills. Rose Ann and fellow guide Richard Webster are now based in their new home in Cave Creek Canyon, Arizona, where they are happily distracted by Bridled Titmice, Acorn Woodpeckers, and a host of hummers.

IF YOU GO

▶ **Getting There:** Most visitors to Podocarpus will fly to Loja, Ecuador, via Quito. Loja is served by TAME, ICARO, and SAEREO Airlines. Quito is served from Miami by LAN Ecuador, Continental, Delta, and American Airlines, among others.

▶ **Best Time to Visit:** Birding in Podocarpus is consistent throughout the year, though February through May is the rainiest period.

▶ **Guides:** All of the major birding tour companies lead trips that include Podocarpus on the itinerary, including Rose Ann's company, Field Guides (800-728-4953; www.fieldguides.com).

▶ **Accommodations:** Copalinga Lodge (+09 347-7013; www.copalinga.com) caters to birders, and is near the Bombuscaro entrance of Podocarpus National Park.

TANDAYAPA-MINDO

RECOMMENDED BY **Kenn Kaufman**

Ecuador has been on the leading edge of ecotourism in South America for decades. Efforts began in the Galápagos, and then extended to eastern Ecuador in the Amazon basin. "Building from these successes, the first bird-specific tourism venues were on the western slopes of the Andes," Kenn Kaufman observed. "It was no longer, 'Come and see the jungle.' It was 'Come and see the hummingbirds.' The Tandayapa-Mindo region has been very well developed for bird watchers."

"My first visit there was in the early nineties. I had been to many different spots in South America, from southern Peru to Venezuela, since the early eighties. There's no question that South America's greatest species diversity rests in the lowlands—from the east base of the Andes trailing out into the Amazon basin. But for some, the spectacular, colorful birds of the mountains—tanagers and hummingbirds among them—hold greater attraction. I guess I fit in that category."

Tandayapa-Mindo is northwest of the Ecuadorian capital of Quito, on the west slope of the Andes in the Choco Endemic Bioregion. It's of mid-level elevation—roughly 6,000 to 7,000 feet. Some of the area's best birding is in close proximity to the Tandayapa Birding Lodge, which offers many trails through adjacent cloud forest habitat.

"One of the birds you'll find here is the Toucan Barbot, one of the most colorful specimens in an assemblage of wildly colored birds," Kenn continued. "If you spend a few days, you're almost guaranteed to see it. Another is the Plate-billed Mountain Toucan, which has bizarre colors—slate blue underneath, a big patch of yellow on the bill, areas of dark chestnut on the chest."

For many, the great attraction of Tandayapa is the hummingbirds. And to experience up to twenty species, you needn't wander farther afield than the lodge's porch. "Tandayapa was one of the first places in the region to put up bird feeders," Kenn continued, "and the results have been impressive. I believe it's changed what we know about hummingbirds; some of the hummers described in Robert Ridgely's book (Birds of Ecuador Field Guide) as being very rare can actually be

seen on the porch quite regularly. The problem is, there are times when you get out on the porch and you don't get any farther. The abundant options, though, are part of the area's appeal. On our last visit, we ran into a group of young, hard-core birders—they were probably hiking twenty miles a day, looking for rare things. We also met an elderly couple that could walk just a bit—they spent most of their time on the deck, watching birds that came in. Tandayapa is an area that can accommodate birders of all skill levels and interests."

It was at Tandayapa that Kenn had the strangest birding experience in his life, a life that has known more than a few strange birding experiences. "While on the east slope of the Andes, we'd heard a story about a man in Tandayapa who had trained a Giant Antpitta to show itself, almost on command, by feeding it worms. Now the Giant Antpitta is a bizarre bird—round-bodied, short-necked, short-tailed, long-legged—it looks like a dingy grapefruit perched atop two soda straws. While antpittas are not terribly difficult to hear if you can whistle an imitation or play a tape recording, they are exceedingly difficult to see. I had seen a few antpittas, but usually it had required an excruciating effort. Among a group of elusive birds, the Giant Antpitta is the most reclusive. Hardly anyone I knew had seen one, though my old friend Ted Parker had.

"The chance to observe the purportedly tamed Giant Antpitta was an offshoot of another small-scale ecotourism project initiated by a Tandayapa farmer and lover of nature named Angel Paz. He owns seventy hectares of land, and had left forty hectares covered with its original growth of subtropical forest. On his property there was a lek (traditional dancing ground) of Andean Cocks-of-the-Rock. The Cock-of-the-Rock is a bird as odd as its name, the size and shape of a football. Males are brilliant flaming orange-red, but in mating season they don't rely on mere color to attract females. Groups of males, a dozen or more, gather at the leks and hop about while they make odd calls. At times, perhaps when a female is nearby, the lek erupts into a frenzy of bobbing and bowing, twanging and growling and squealing.

"Mr. Paz reasoned that the many birding tourists who came to the area might be willing to pay to watch these birds, generating some extra income to help support his family. So he set out to make a good trail through the forest from his house to the lek. One day as he was working on cutting the trail, he noticed a large, plump, gray-brown bird lurking nearby. He didn't know its name but he knew it was a ground-dweller with a haunting, hooting voice, a shy bird, hard to approach. But this individual was only a few yards away. Paz's shovel had just turned up an earthworm, and on a whim, he tossed the worm to the lurking bird. Instead of running away, the bird bounded forward on its long legs and swallowed the worm. Paz took on the challenge of winning the trust of this shy forest bird. He would watch for it every day, and if he could approach close

OPPOSITE:
A Giant Antpitta, a welcome suprise for birders visiting Tandayapa.

79

enough, he would toss a worm to it. The bird learned to associate Mr. Paz with these morsels, and eventually it would come when he called—he had named it Manuel—to grab a handout before vanishing into the forest undergrowth.

"Mr. Paz had not abandoned his plan to bring birding tourists to see the Andean Cocks-of-the-Rock, and after contacting the local birding lodges, he had his first group of visitors. The birders enjoyed watching the lek, and as they were on their way out, Mr. Paz thought they might be interested to see Manuel, his shy forest bird. But they were a lot more than merely interested. The visitors went berserk to see a Giant Antpitta.

"We finally were able to meet Mr. Paz, and after a nerve-wracking drive up a slick dirt road, we were walking the trail to the observation blind to watch the Cocks-of-the-Rock displaying and showing off at first light. Amazing and spectacular they were, a fitting warm-up act. Meanwhile, his son had brought a dish of earthworms dug up elsewhere on the farm. Stopping by a stream, Mr. Paz explained that he had to wash these worms before offering them to Manuel. After twenty minutes (it was more like a baptism than a washing), he led us slowly down the trail. My curiosity had reached a fever pitch, wondering what would happen next. The forest had been relatively quiet in the rain on this morning, with few bird calls, and even now that the rain had stopped I had not heard anything that sounded like an antpitta. Where we were standing there was no sign of any bird. 'Manuel!' Mr. Paz shouted suddenly, and I jumped; it was the first time we had heard him raise his voice. 'Manuel! Venga, venga!' (Come, come!) 'Venga, venga, venga, Manuel!'

"Yeah, right, I said to myself. This had to be some kind of practical joke. But looking into his face, it was clear he was not joking. Mr. Paz was peering with a deep intensity at a spot in the dense undergrowth alongside the trail ahead . . . a spot where a hulking shape lurked among the foliage. It had come silently and it was barely visible, a darker shadow among shadows, and then it was gone again. But we knew something had been there. Mr. Paz knew it too. 'Manuel,' he said, more quietly now. 'Manuel! Venga.'

"And before our unbelieving eyes, Manuel did come. The bird hopped out into the open, out into the center of the muddy trail. Manuel was a big bird, and a weird-looking one as well, with a punched-in bill, fat neck, big eyes, and squiggles of black on its rusty belly. Some might call it ugly. For us, it was beautiful.

"We were frozen where we stood, but Mr. Paz crept forward a couple of steps and then gently tossed an earthworm out onto the trail. The Giant Antpitta cocked its head, bounded forward with great springy hops, grabbed the worm, and retreated into the undergrowth. A few moments later it reappeared, coming closer this time. Mr. Paz fed the antpitta three more times, and for one of these worms the bird came up to only a few inches away from his outstretched hand. But it never lost its furtive look, and after four worms it melted away silently into the forest."

KENN KAUFMAN is an author, artist, teacher, traveler, and naturalist who has focused on birds since the age of six. Two of his books, A Field Guide to Advanced Birding and Lives of North American Birds, are now considered standard references for birders. Kenn's Kingbird Highway has been hailed as "one of the best books ever written about birding." In 2000, Houghton Mifflin Company launched Kenn's new field guide series, Kaufman Focus Guides, with a brand new guide to all North American birds. The series now includes volumes on North American butterflies (2003) and mammals (2004). He has led nature tours on six continents, and has been responsible for developing Victor Emmanuel Nature Tours' program of educational birding workshops.

IF YOU GO

➤ **Getting There:** Tandayapa Valley is an hour and a half from Quito along a good paved road, making it one of Ecuador's more accessible birding hotspots. Quito is served from Miami by LAN Ecuador, Continental, Delta, and American Airlines, among others.

➤ **Best Time to Visit:** Birding can be best at the outset of the rainy season (before the rains get too heavy), from October to February.

➤ **Guides:** Tandayapa Bird Lodge (below) has local guides available.

➤ **Accommodations:** Tandayapa Bird Lodge (+593 2-244-7520; www.tandayapa.com) is one of the preferred accommodations in the region, and is convenient to Mr. Paz and Manuel.

CLEY NEXT THE SEA

RECOMMENDED BY **Bryan Bland**

Among British birders, there's a saying that goes "Everything comes to Cley." Everything, including Bryan Bland, who took residence in a local flint-and-brick house built in 1500 (with a new wing added in 1780!) at Cley Next the Sea to be close to Great Britain's most renowned birding locale.

"There's no question that this is where birding began," Bryan said. "There are written bird records for Norfolk going back over one thousand years. In those days, birds weren't written up as we chronicle them today. Instead, there were inventories of birds that were captured and eaten at wedding banquets and the like. Bird notes as we understand them emerged in the 1600s. I remember coming across a letter written by Sir Thomas Browne, physician to Charles I, antiquarian and notable literary figure, while I was doing some research. He had come to Norfolk to be near the birds, and in his letter he said:

> Beside the ordinarie birds which keep constantly in the country many are discoverable both in winter and summer which are of a migrant nature and exchange their seats according to the season. Those which come in the spring coming for the most part from the southward, those which come in the autumn or winter from the northward. So that they are observed to come in great flocks with a north east wind and to depart with a south west. Nor to come only in flocks of one kind butt teals, woodcocks, feltars, thrushes, and small birds to come and light together, for the most part some hawkes and birds of pray attending them.

"This reads just like a paragraph from the current Cley Bird Club Report. Sir Thomas had got it spot-on; he understood migration a hundred years before Gilbert White (who was no fool) was debating whether swallows hibernated in the mud."

Cley Next the Sea is in the heart of East Anglia, in the county of Norfolk. It was once the second-busiest port on the east coast of England, but its importance has been in decline since

OPPOSITE:

The windmill at Cley Next the Sea is one of the most painted and photographed sites in England.

1300. Now it's an attractive village—flint cottages with Flemish gable ends, plus the most photographed and painted windmill in the world.

The region seems tailor-made for attracting avian life. "Looking at a map, you'll notice that East Anglia bulges out into the North Sea," Bryan continued. "Cley and Blakeney Point are halfway along the coast, where it falls away, both to the west and the east. The shingle spit is like an arm with beckoning fingers, attracting birds on migration to and from Scandinavia, or across from the Netherlands. Cley is the first landfall for many birds—from finches to raptors. Beyond its geographic position, Cley offers a variety of ideal habitats. There's farmland and woodland, marshes and reed beds, lagoons and hedgerows. There's plenty to support many resident birds, as well as lots of extras. It's not just good in winter or good in summer or good at migration times. There's something exciting going on every single day of the year. This February day, there's a Glaucous Gull on the beach feeding on a dead seal with flocks of Snow Buntings nearby, a thousand Common and Velvet Scoters offshore, Avocets and Black-tailed Godwits on the scrapes, and Marsh Harriers and Bearded Tits in the reedbed. In fact, of all the species illustrated on the dust jacket of The Birds of Norfolk, only the Black Tern is not present at Cley today."

Beyond its abundance of native birds and England's best chance to come upon a rarity ("Everything comes to Cley"), Cley radiates a homey appeal that's as attractive to Londoners as it is to birders from abroad. "The reserve at Cley is the oldest county wildlife trust reserve in England, which would likely make it the oldest in the world," Bryan said. "People used to come here to shoot birds. They'd stay at the George Inn or rent a houseboat, then head off with ten-bore guns or pumt guns mounted on boats, shooting hundreds of birds at a time. That changed nearly a hundred years ago, when the Cley Marsh came up for sale. A far-sighted doctor named Sydney Long lobbied to buy the marsh to prevent people from shooting over it. He recognized that if habitat wasn't preserved, the breeding birds would decline. At the time, the Bittern, Avocet, Marsh Harrier, and Bearded Tit had already been lost as British breeding birds. The Cley Marsh was purchased, then Hickling Broad (a shallow lake formed by a flooded medieval peat dig) and a number of other properties as the conservation movement gained momentum. An auctioneer at the time was said to have quipped, 'Would that all England were under water,' as bird habitat was claiming bigger prices than prime agricultural land. Since that time, all of the species that had been lost have recolonized from the Netherlands. Happily, the entire Norfolk coast for twenty miles either side of Cley, and much of the county inland, is now preserved.

"I've led over 1,000 tours around the world, but still derive the most pleasure from my residential courses at Cley. Guests always comment on the pleasant attitude of the residents. Life here is very much like life was a hundred years ago, or even five hundred years ago. There's still time for people. If I stop in a lane to look at birds on a hedge, I'll become aware that there's a car or several cars behind me, but they don't toot. They wait patiently. Even the meter maids and men—hated figures in most places—are good-natured. A few years back, I had taken some folks to Yarmouth, as we'd heard there was a Mediterranean Gull there. I was out on the beach with the group, and a parking-meter man came up and asked, 'Is that your white minibus?' I said 'Yes.' He replied, 'I've been looking all over for you, as you've forgotten to put a ticket on it. But I'm only on for another half hour and no one else will be coming on in my stead, so if you just pay for half an hour, you can stay all day.' I pointed out that we had only come to see the Mediterranean Gull and were about to leave. 'Oh, then you'll not need a ticket,' he said. 'Sorry to have bothered you.'"

From his house in Cley, Bryan Bland has assembled one of Great Britain's greatest window lists. "I remember one occasion in 1982 when a Little Whimbrel turned up in South Wales, coinciding with a Long-toed Stint in the Northeast," Bryan continued. "There had never been a Little Whimbrel in Great Britain before and I guessed that there would never be another, so I opted to drive west. Three years later I saw one from my window, the only one that's ever been seen in England; I still haven't seen a Long-toed Stint, but one will come to Cley eventually! In the winter of 2003, I had a slipped disc and sciatica. I was really poleaxed, but it proved fortunate. On February 21, I saw a Pallid Harrier—a Central Palearctic species—from my window. If I'd been well, I'd certainly not have been at home. I would venture that mine is one of the few windows in Great Britain that's been afforded views of all four Western Palearctic harriers. And then there was the time when there was word of a Ferruginous Duck on the borrow pit just beyond the new flood bank. I couldn't see over the bank from my top-floor window, so I cut a hole in my roof. After I spotted it, I had to install a Velux roof light."

Bryan shared another story that captures all the gentle charm of Cley and its inhabitants. "About thirty years ago, I was out on the heath photographing warblers and a Red-footed Falcon, near a place called The Hangs, which is private land. There I learned that someone had seen a Rose-colored Starling on the grounds—a rare bird in these parts. The owner had sworn me to secrecy, as he didn't want a mass of birders on his land. This put me in an awkward spot: We have a code in Norfolk, and it's 'suppress no secrets.' I felt compelled to put this piece of information out, yet in doing so, I would have to betray the landowner, who'd shared a confidence.

"As it turned out, I was saved from the betrayal. When I got home, a lady in the village called to report that a funny bird was in her garden. After a few questions, it was confirmed that the bird was the Rose-colored Starling. I told her it was a very rare bird, and asked if it would be okay for people to come by. She said 'Certainly.' I warned her that it would be not several people, but hundreds of people. She said, 'Oh, that's fine.'

"She worked out a system to please the bird and its observers. To keep the bird content, she fed it chips for a week. People waited at the roadside for the feeding to occur. Once she'd fed it chips and the bird had come down into her garden, she'd run to the street and tell people that it had come in. I was concerned that the crowds were becoming a bother. 'Are you sure you're not harassed?' I asked. She said 'No, they're a wonderful crowd. They've been here a week and haven't even left one piece of litter.'

"This lady and her husband were great fans of the actor John Wayne, who by coincidence had died that very week. As a small thank you, I carved and painted a little wooden sign for the cottage—which they called 'Western Cottage'—showing their hero riding into the sunset."

DESTINATION 17

BRYAN BLAND has been fascinated by natural history, and in particular birds, for as long as he can remember, but it was not until 1974 that he decided to resign his directorships to pioneer a new style of residential bird watching course in Norfolk. His original methods combined with his ability to caricature the diagnostic points of any species quickly, led him to be regarded as one of the leading teachers in practical ornithology. These courses are alternated with birding trips abroad which Bryan leads as a director of Sunbird Tours (www.sunbirdtours.co.uk). His "Birds and Music" and "Birds and History" combinations (reflecting other interests outside ornithology) have become very popular. Bryan has watched birds in over fifty countries around the world, including some in North, Central, and South America; North and East Africa; Asia and throughout Europe. Bryan is much in demand as a lecturer. He has been responsible, over the last quarter century, for directly and personally enthusing thousands of today's birdwatchers, with many more through broadcasts on radio and television. Bryan's interest in identification is evinced by the fact that he has served on the records committees of both Norfolk and Scilly and has over the last thirty years discovered numerous rarities. To date he has seen 380 species in Norfolk, 334 of them in the Cley area, and his window list has passed the 200 mark. Bryan retains an interest in and love of his common birds. He is also well known as an illustrator, his first published drawings appearing when he was two years old. More recently, there have been numerous illustrations for several books and magazines. Britain's first breeding Parrot Crossbills used trimmings from Bryan's beard when nesting at Wells in 1984.

➤ **Getting There:** Cley Next the Sea is roughly three hours' drive north of London, in North Norfolk.

➤ **Best Time to Visit:** Like any great birding spot, Cley and North Norfolk have something going on year-round. Fall and spring are high times for migration.

➤ **Guides:** Bryan Bland offers tours when he's at home. To arrange for a memorable day of birding, write Bryan at: Flanders, High Street, Cley-Next-the-Sea, Holt, Norfolk, NR25 7RB; or, call +44 1263 740803. North Norfolk Birds (+44 1263 711396; www.northnorfolkbirds.co.uk) also provides guiding services.

➤ **Accommodations:** The Cley Next the Sea community website (www.cley.org.uk) lists lodging options in Cley.

17

DESTINATION

ST. MARKS NATIONAL WILDLIFE REFUGE

RECOMMENDED BY **Don Morrow**

On March 31, 1933, President Roosevelt signed the Emergency Conservation Work Act into law, effectively putting 250,000 young men to work around a nation in the throes of the Great Depression. Members of what would come to be called the Civilian Conservation Corps (CCC) planted trees to prevent erosion, built trails and facilities in what would become a burgeoning system of public parks (711, all told), and erected many of the landmark lodges that grace America's national parks. And they helped create at least one migratory-bird sanctuary—St. Marks Refuge.

"A lot of the habitat along the northern section of the Gulf Coast is very similar," Don Morrow began. "It's what might be termed a low-energy coast line—miles of salt marsh and salt flats, little in the way of beaches. St. Marks Refuge is very different. Once the land had been set aside, the CCC came in and constructed a road into the salt marsh, and an interconnected series of dikes, all to establish pools that would provide habitat for wintering ducks. While such wetlands manipulation would never be allowed today, the project has been incredibly successful. Waterfowl come each winter in droves, and the dikes give birders miles of walking access to an area that would otherwise be inaccessible."

St. Marks Refuge is a sprawling preserve of 68,000 acres spanning three northwest Florida counties along the Gulf Coast. It includes four operating units—St. Marks, Wakulla, Panacea, and Aucilla. The St. Marks unit is of greatest interest to birders, offering access to the fresh- and salt-water impoundments mentioned above, as well as upland forest habitat and the open waters of Apalachee Bay. A seven-mile road winds through this unit, ending near the current St. Marks Lighthouse, which was built in 1866 (after the previous lighthouse was abandoned thanks to mining by Confederate soldiers). More than 270 species have been observed at St. Marks, including such rarities as Mongolian Plover. ("That plover had birders jetting in from as far away as Chicago!" Don exclaimed.) But it's wintering ducks that people primarily come for. "You may have fifteen or sixteen species of waterfowl on a given pool on a good day," Don continued. "Sometimes rafts of thousands of ducks come through. The dikes allow people to get very close. We get some Western migrants, too, in the early winter—Vermillion Flycatchers, Western Kingbirds. It's as though they were heading south, hit the Gulf of Mexico and said, 'Do we head right or left for Central America? Maybe it's left.' It's not uncommon to have hundred-species days at St. Marks."

For some visiting birders, St. Marks Refuge is an end in itself. For others, it's just the beginning. St. Marks is one of the gateways for the Great Florida Birding Trail, a program created by the Florida Fish and Wildlife Conservation Commission, the Florida Department of Transportation, and the Florida Wildlife Foundation. The trail maps out 445 birding sites along 2,000 miles of highway in the Sunshine State, and gives visitors an excellent point of reference for locating Florida's 495 native species, including the Florida Burrowing Owl and the Florida Scrub-Jay.

An ideal winter day at St. Marks begins just before dawn. "I like to drive along the entrance road, looking for Woodcocks and Whippoorwills," Don said. "The Whippoorwills don't call then, but in the stands of pine along the entrance road, you're likely to hear Great Horned Owls, which are very vocal right at dawn. With early light, we'll often get a morning flight of herons—Great Blue and Little Blue, Tri-colored, and Black-crowned Night. There might be some White Ibis mixed in, and occasionally Wood Stork, Glossy Ibis, and Roseate Spoonbills. Once the morning flight is over, we'll walk out on the dikes to look for ducks. Quite a range of species is possible, including Blue-winged Teal and Black Ducks. Snow Geese and Greater White-fronted Geese are also possible. If the tide is heading out, it would be the best time for spotting shorebirds—Western Sandpiper, Long- and Short-billed Dowitchers, American Oystercatchers, Long-billed Curlew, and Marbled Godwit. If the tide is high, you'll want to be out by the lighthouse, where you'll get Bufflehead, Common Loon, Red-throated Loon on occasion, perhaps Scoters and Long-tailed Duck, too. All the while, we'll be on the lookout for Bald Eagles. We have some breeding pairs at St. Marks—they're here for the same reason as the birders, the ducks. If you notice ducks moving, there's probably an eagle around."

The Florida sun that can be oppressive and punishing in July has a gentler mien in the winter, as Don can attest. "In late afternoon on a February or March day, high-pressure systems will move in from the Gulf, with blue skies spreading from horizon to horizon. Long golden rays of sun illuminate the salt-marsh vegetation, turning it a light golden brown, a contrast to the dark green of the islands of pine on the land. I've been out there after dark watching the sky. Black thunderheads float out on the Gulf with lightning flashing inside, lighting them up like Chinese lanterns. Though St. Marks is a popular destination for Tallahassee residents, you can have those amazing skies all to yourself out on the dikes. You have the feeling of leaving everything and everyone behind."

DON MORROW received his undergraduate degree from the University of Florida and his master's degree in Environmental Studies from Antioch University. He has worked as a field biologist and as a naturalist for Morningside Nature Center in Gainesville and for the Audubon Society of New Hampshire. An avid birder since childhood, Don has led field trips locally for Birdsong Nature Center, Apalachee Audubon Society, and the St. Marks National Wildlife Refuge. For the last twenty years he has worked for the Trust for Public Land as a senior project manager with TPL's Southeast Regional Office in Tallahassee, Florida. Don has primary responsibility for the Trust's efforts in Louisiana, Mississippi, Alabama, and Arkansas. Over the past twenty-three years, he has completed land preservation projects that have resulted in the preservation of over 55,000 acres of land. Don has worked with federal, state, and local governments on projects ranging from conservation easements on urban greenways to the acquisition of inholdings in National Forest wilderness areas.

IF YOU GO

➤ **Getting There:** St. Marks National Wildlife Refuge is twenty-five miles south of Tallahassee, which is served by Delta, Northwest, and U.S. Airways.
➤ **Best Time to Visit:** Winter months offer the greatest species diversity and the best weather.
➤ **Guides:** St. Marks National Wildlife Refuge (www.fws.gov/saintmarks/) has resources for self-guided tours. Don Morrow occasionally leads tours as a volunteer.
➤ **Accommodations:** Tallahassee Area Convention and Visitors Bureau online Visitor Guide (www.visittallahassee.com).

THULE

RECOMMENDED BY **Kurt K. Burnham**

While some may look upon Greenland and see an icy wasteland, others see vitality and even magic. "I'm fascinated by Arctic landscapes and by falcons," Kurt Burnham said. "I like to go back and read old books on the Arctic. There aren't too many places where you can read the old books, go to the place that's referenced—and find it still intact as it was described. In 2002, while we were conducting research on Greenland, we visited the area where Admiral Robert Peary had based his expeditions in the 1890s. Everything was as it had been—even the old railroad ties that were used to load things on the boat. It's as if they had just loaded a few days before our arrival and left. It's so cold in those parts, things decompose very slowly."

Greenland (which is administrated by Denmark) is the largest island in the world, covering almost 840,000 square miles of predominantly ice, glacier, and tundra; it's three times the size of Texas. Scientists place the ice cap in some places at over 16,000 feet (10,000 feet above the sea, 6,000 feet below); two-thirds of the landmass is perpetually covered in permafrost. There are just over 50,000 residents in all of Greenland—mostly of Inuit descent with a smattering of Danes—and mostly scattered along the island's mountainous coastline, where the only exposed land occurs. Thule is situated on the northwest coast of Greenland near Baffin Bay, 695 miles north of the Arctic Circle and 950 miles south of the North Pole. The name "Thule" is derived from a Latin word that translates as "northernmost part of the inhabitable world." (Those with warm-weather constitutions might debate the "inhabitable" part!) The main man-made feature of Thule is a U.S. Air Force base, established in 1951. In addition to pilots, the valley where Thule rests between North and South Mountains is home to arctic fox, hares, polar bears, caribou, seals, musk ox, and several species of birds—including Gyrfalcons and Peregrine Falcons. "Greenlanders have generally been hard on their environment, in terms of extractive industries and overhunting," Kurt continued. "In many areas in Greenland, specifically the central-west and southwest where large

91

human populations are present, significant declines in many species of birds have been observed, including the complete extirpation of several species over large areas. The Thule area has one of the largest intact ecosystems left in Greenland, with an abundant amount of bird and marine life, primarily as a result of the small number of human inhabitants."

Thule—and Greenland in general—are not likely to become the focal point of birding tour-company activities anytime soon. "The ice around Thule doesn't break up until mid to late July," Kurt said, "and there aren't regular commercial flights. Almost every month of the year, you'll have hundred-mile-per-hour winds; the highest winds ever recorded reached at least 225 knots; the weather equipment eventually blew away! It's not uncommon to have snow, even in the summer." Yet amongst these rugged conditions, there's an incredible profusion of life. "Huge numbers of Alcids breed in this area—thirty to sixty million birds," Kurt continued. "The Dovekie colonies are amazing; they nest in the talus slopes along the coast. You can lie on your back for twenty-four hours looking up, and there will always be birds flying over. Near the breeding grounds, the guano smell is very profound. I'll take a jacket out of storage two years after being in Greenland, and it will still have that smell."

Another Greenland birding attraction is the colony of Thick-billed Murres on Saunders Island, off the northeastern coast. "The colony—over one million birds—nests on a section of cliffs several miles long," Kurt continued. "It's solid birds, from five or ten feet off the water to 800 feet up. There are no nests; the birds find a crack or tiny ledge along the cliffs and line up, holding their egg on their feet. Their eggs are uniquely shaped. Most eggs are oval or round-shaped, and will roll. A murre egg is flat on one end, skinny on the other. If you were to roll it, it rotates in a tight circle. When the murre moves, the egg stays in one place instead of rolling off of the ledge."

If there's one bird that's representative of Greenland, it's the Gyrfalcon. (Gyrfalcons are, in fact, the official bird of neighboring Iceland.) This bird of prey—the largest in the falcon family, with a wingspan over four feet—has held a mystique for humans since medieval times, when they were considered "the bird of Kings" in Europe (this due largely to issues of supply and demand). "When you hear of people paying a 'King's ransom,'" Kurt said, "part of the ransom was very likely a Gyrfalcon." The sparse terrain of Thule is ideally suited for these birds, which feed primarily on ptarmigan and, where available, small rodents. "You'll see Gyrfalcons in other parts of Greenland in several colors, including black, white, and gray," Kurt continued. "But in Thule only white Gyrs exist, which is what birders want to see. The whitest Gyrs in the world are found in Thule and other areas in the far north of Greenland. In May, when they begin nesting, you can only make out their heads, as the rest of their body is in the snow."

DESTINATION 19

OPPOSITE:
The window for visiting Greenland is mid-July through August, when the ice around the land mass briefly breaks up.

Recently Kurt has been the project leader on the first long-term satellite radio telemetry study of Gyrfalcons and Peregrine Falcons in Thule. The transmitters will allow the team to monitor the daily movements of the falcons for over a year. "No one really knows where Gyrfalcons from the west coast of Greenland spend the winter months," Kurt continued. "It's unlikely they stay in their breeding territories because of the three months of absolute darkness during winter. They may migrate to southern Greenland or Canada or even winter on the ice and feed on wintering seabird populations." Data gathered from the study will help biologists from the Peregrine Fund determine geographic areas of importance for conservation of falcons in the future.

KURT K. BURNHAM has been involved with the Peregrine Fund his entire life. The son of Bill and Pat Burnham, Kurt's passion for falcons started at a young age helping to raise imprint falcons at home. Kurt first went to Greenland in 1991 and has returned every year since. He started working at the World Center for Birds of Prey, doing odd jobs around the facility in 1990. In 1997 Kurt graduated from Albertson College of Idaho with a B.S. in biology. By 1998 Kurt was appointed the Greenland Project Manager. In 2000 Kurt became a full-time employee of the Peregrine Fund and also its Arctic Projects director. In 2001 Kurt was accepted at the University of Oxford, United Kingdom, and began work on his Ph.D., the focus of his thesis being falcon research in Greenland. He divides his time between Greenland, Idaho, and England, spending about a third of the year in each. When not out of the country, Kurt is an avid outdoorsman and thoroughly enjoys upland bird hunting, specifically for chukars, with his dogs Zeus and Zoke. He also spends his free time big-game hunting, fly fishing, scuba diving, and boating.

IF YOU GO

➤ **Getting There:** Thule is not an easy place to get to. Air Greenland serves Kangerlussuaq from Baltimore; from there, flights are available to Qaanaaq (which is north of Thule). Once in Qaanaaq, you can hire local boats to take you into the field (through Hotel Qaanaaq).

➤ **Best Time to Visit:** The window for visiting Thule is small—mid-July to mid-September.

➤ **Guides:** No birding specific guides are available around Thule. However, the Peregrine Fund is always seeking volunteers to assist with fieldwork (volunteers would need to pay their own way and make a donation). Contact Kurt Burnham at kburnham@higharctic.org.

➤ **Accommodations:** Hotel Qaanaaq (+29 997-1234) can accommodate small parties.

THE HIGHLANDS

RECOMMENDED BY **Bill Thompson, III**

Guatemala might be called the Rodney Dangerfield of Central American birding—it just doesn't get the respect it deserves. After all, Guatemala boasts nineteen different ecosystems, from mangrove swamps to lowland jungles to high woodlands, attracting winter migrants from North America and northbound birds from South America, in addition to its own residents. In total, some 700 species have been recorded in Guatemala.

Much of this lack of recognition has to do with the on-again/off-again revolution/civil war that tore at the country for nearly fifty years; travelers wary of such potential dangers were unlikely to come upon a Horned Guan. Furthermore—and to Guatemala's great consternation—those who did venture to see the great ruins at Tikal (in the northeastern section of the country) generally did so via Belize or the Yucatán, only seeing a fragment of what the nation had to offer . . . and failing to leave many tourist dollars behind. "Guatemalans see the 'hit and run' that many visitors do on Tikal as the equivalent of traveling to the U.S. and only visiting Disney World," Bill Thompson said. "I agree. Going to Guatemala and only visiting Tikal would be dismissive. Though I will say there was some fantastic birding around there, even right amidst the ancient temples."

In 1998, a peace accord was struck between warring factions, and shortly thereafter, the nation of Guatemala sought to announce to the ecotourism world that it was open for business. "I was invited to visit Guatemala by a tourism agency along with a bunch of other bird-writing people, as part of an effort to rehabilitate the country's image," Bill continued. "On that first trip, only the very adventurous went. We were given a very nice tour, though we didn't get to some of the more remote areas I'd hoped we'd visit. Still, I was impressed. The places we visited were still very unspoiled; the government had been far-sighted in setting aside large tracts of land. And the Guatemalan people were very eager to show off their country. I had the sense that the people were thrilled that someone like myself had taken the effort to come visit them.

Bill was encouraged enough to return to Guatemala on a longer trip, this time with his wife, Julie Zickefoose. On this trip, he was able to get a bit more off the beaten path in a nation that had been off the beaten path for gringos for half a century. The Highlands region—formed by mountain ranges that cross from west to east near the bottom third of the country with peaks reaching nearly 14,000 feet—was especially captivating. "This region of Guatemala is home to three very special birds, a trifecta of *rara avis*: the Horned Guan, the Resplendent Quetzal, and the Pink-headed Warbler. The area is gorgeous—beautiful blue lakes surrounded by active volcanoes," Bill continued. "We did a great deal of hiking, as you might imagine. The first memorable hike was up Volcan San Pedro, in an effort to see Horned Guan.

"Horned Guan is a species of tree-dwelling, chicken-like bird, but much weirder. They're very secretive by nature, and even more so, as they taste good and have been actively hunted in many areas. On Volcan San Pedro, there's a park that's been set aside for them. You hike and hike and hike—you're up thousands of feet and the trails are very steep. Our Guatemalan hosts were huffing and puffing slightly. The Americans in the group could barely put one foot in front of the other. Meanwhile, the local farmers were trotting past us as they went up and down to their mountainside farming plots. We had a police escort—I guess because we were considered VIPs. It was the police, who were hiking ahead of us, who found the bird, high up in a tree. We got the word by walkie-talkie. I never have exerted myself so much in my life as I did the last 150 yards to where the Guan was perched. My friend Alvaro helped me the last five feet up; I nearly blacked out. But I got my scope up, and there it was, looking very much like a dinosaur. It was a fantastic experience, made all the better by the effort it took to get there."

Bill's quest for the Guatemalan Trifecta continued. "I had always wanted to see a Resplendent Quetzal (Guatemala's national bird, and the name of the national currency). They're a member of the trogon family; the scapular feathers of the males can reach two feet. On my first trip, we'd gone to the eastern cloud forest to see it. We heard one, but couldn't see it in the fog and rain. This time around, a special trip had been arranged for me in the western cloud forest, near Los Andes. A lot of shade-grown coffee and tea is grown here, and there are Resplendent Quetzals in nesting boxes. We heard one, and soon after I spotted it." Two down, one to go.

"The last member of the trifecta was the Pink-headed Warbler, another highland bird. They're not merely pink, but a frosty pink; these warblers look like a pink snow cone. They're very curious birds. Once you find them, you can call them in. Our quest for the Pink-headed Warbler took us up the side of Volcan Chicabal. As we made our way up, villagers were passing us en route to the lake in the caldera of the volcano, which they consider sacred; they were going to perform their

OPPOSITE: Mountains in the Highlands reach heights of 14,000 feet, and include several active volcanoes.

20

DESTINATION

spring ritual, to ask for rain. The farmers were very curious that we were there just to look at birds.

"We saw the Pink-headed Warblers, and began making our way down. Of course, the farmers we'd seen earlier passed us again. One of the farmers asked, 'Did you see your beautiful birds?' We said yes. They said, 'Thank you. We prayed for you.'"

BILL THOMPSON, III, is the editor of Bird Watcher's Digest, the popular bimonthly magazine that has been published by his family since 1978. An avid bird watcher from the age of eight, Bill knew that birds would someday become the focus of his career. Bill worked as a professional musician and was a senior account executive at Ogilvy & Mather in New York prior to joining Bird Watcher's Digest. Bill is the author of Bird Watching for Dummies, The Backyard Bird Watcher's Answer Guide, and An Identification Guide to Backyard Birds. Bill edits the Backyard Booklet Series for Bird Watcher's Digest. This series includes thirteen titles and has sold more than 5 million copies since its inception. He is also the author of eighteen state bird books in the Bird Watching: A Year-Round Guide series from Cool Springs Press, and he is the lead author of Identify Yourself: Birding's 50 Most Common ID Challenges (2005) from Houghton Mifflin, which is illustrated by his wife, artist/author Julie Zickefoose. Bill has given keynote presentations at more than forty birding events since 1998. Bill is a director of the Ohio Ornithological Society and a longtime member of the American Birding Association. He has trekked to many of the great birding hotspots in Europe, Africa, the Middle East, and Central America. Bill still plays guitar with several bands—Chick Sandwich, and The Swinging Orangutans, which includes his wife, Julie, and his brother Andy.

IF YOU GO

➤ **Getting There:** Most visitors will fly into Guatemala City, which is in the Highlands region, and is served by many major carriers, including American, Continental, and Delta.

➤ **Best Time to Visit:** Most Highlands specialty birds are present year-round. November to April are the coolest and driest months; July to September are the wettest.

➤ **Guides:** Organized birding is nascent in Guatemala, but local tour companies are emerging, including Cayaya Birding (+50 25-308-5160; www.cayaya-birding.com) and Aventuras Naturales (+50 25-381-6615; http://aventurasnaturales.tripod.com).

➤ **Accommodations:** Bill recommends Los Andes (www.andescloudforest.com), Los Tarrales (+50 22-478-4867; www.tarrales.com) and Finca Patrocinio (+50 25-203-5701).

KAUAI

RECOMMENDED BY **Bob Sundstrom**

Kauai is known—at least in promotional literature—as "The Garden Isle." As it turns out, sometimes travel brochures do not distort the truth. Much of the island is incredibly lush, and this quality helps make Kauai a desirable habitat for a number of seabirds and forest birds you're not likely to see back home.

"A number of things come together to make Kauai a wonderful birding experience, and a wonderful tourist experience," began Bob Sundstrom, who's led more than thirty birding tours to the island. "The best birding sites are very accessible. While the Big Island (Hawaii) may have higher diversity, you have to cover a lot more ground to find the birds. Kauai is small enough that you can cover all the best spots in a few days, from one base, without extensive driving. It's only one and a half hours to the farthest point (Kokee State Forest) from the east shore, where we stay in a pleasant hotel on the beach. On Kauai, you can take a very productive birding boat trip, and squeeze in some fine snorkeling, too. When I first started doing tours on Kauai, I'd get some hardcore listers who wanted to bird dawn to dark. Increasingly, I get people who are enchanted with the idea of going to Hawaii and taking full advantage of its unique and varied tropical forests and coastal regions, rather than the prepackaged Hawaii of golf courses and condominiums."

Kauai is the oldest of the eight islands that make up the Hawaiian archipelago, which is the most remote archipelago in the world; this last fact may often be forgotten, thanks to the ubiquity of the aforementioned prepackaged vacations, which make the islands seem much closer than they are. Hawaii boasts the world's largest proportion of endemic plant and animal species; it would be very rare indeed for a nonnative bird species to find their way here, 2,500 miles from any continental landmass. Kauai's defining physical characteristic is Wai'ale'ale, a volcanic peak that rises from the center of this mountainous island. While not Kauai's highest mountain, Wai'ale'ale is responsible for capturing the moisture that makes the east side of the island one of the wettest

places on earth, recording an average annual rainfall of 476 inches. In addition to supplementing Kauai's rich flora, eons of rain have created some incredibly dramatic canyon landscapes, including Waimea Canyon, which Mark Twain once dubbed "the Grand Canyon of the Pacific." "The tropical scenery is just magical," Bob continued. "Just about wherever you are on the island, the lush, emerald green, highly contoured highlands are in view."

OPPOSITE:
A Laysan Albatross nestling at Kilauea Point on Kauai.

There are a number of birding hotspots on Kauai, but of two Bob's favorites capture both the avian and scenic appeal of the island. The first is Kilauea Point National Wildlife Refuge, the northernmost point in the Hawaiian Islands. This 300-acre refuge consists of rolling hillsides and coastal cliffs, and is widely considered the best place to see Kauai's signature seabirds. "Red-tailed and White-tailed Tropicbirds are very common at Kilauea," Bob said. "On several occasions, I've been lucky enough to see a Red-billed Tropicbird among a group of Red-taileds. The Red-tailed is one of the most beautiful birds in the world, almost too good to be true. At Kilauea, you can see the tropicbirds at very close range, as you're on a cliff about a hundred feet up from the surf, and the birds catch updrafts and hover right in front of you."

There's a host of interesting species at Kilauea, including Great Frigatebirds, Red-footed Boobies, Brown Boobies, Hawaiian Petrels, Wedge-tailed and Newell's Shearwaters, and Nene (the state bird of Hawaii). But for many birders, the most sought-after species here is the Laysan Albatross, which nests on the refuge. "In the winter months, you can scope the nests from a hundred yards away and see huge gray nestlings in the shade of ironwood trees," Bob added. "It's amazing to get that close to nesting albatross, outside of the Galápagos or Antarctica." One of Bob's most enduring memories of Kilauea was the courtship display of a pair of Red-tailed Tropicbirds. "These birds do a fascinating display—they hang in the air, one above the other, and rotate in a kind of backward circle. We were on the edge of the headlands, looking out at these beautiful white-and-red birds standing out in relief against the blue of the Pacific."

For forest-oriented species, Bob will take his clients to Kokee State Park, on the northwestern side of the island. The 4,345-acre park rests at an altitude between 3,200 and 4,200 feet, and encompasses one of Kauai's most dramatic landmarks, Waimea Canyon. The canyon is a mile wide, ten miles long, and over 3,500 feet deep. "When we go to Kokee, we always leave time to view the canyon," Bob continued. "From some vantage points, you get the copper colors of the canyon and the greens of Kalalau Valley—sometimes contrasted by White-tailed Tropicbirds sailing around—it's the very image of a tropical paradise." The best birding takes place in the lush forests of koa and ohia. "In Kokee, you'll find species that are endemic to Hawaii, like the Hawaiian Honeycreeper, and some that are endemic to Kauai alone. These would include Apapanes, a red

21

DESTINATION

honeycreeper the size of a sparrow that sits in the blossoms of ohia, possessing a wonderful, irregular song. Other endemics here are the Anianiau and Kauai Amakihi, little green or yellow birds the size of warblers, and Elepaio, which is related to Old World flycatchers, and reminiscent of a wren or chickadee.

"After hiking around Kokee, you can drive down the access road and you'll end up at an overlook at the Na Pali Cliffs. If you're lucky, you'll be there when it's free of clouds. The view down the steep, concave slopes to the Pacific is breathtaking. I was up there once watching some White-tailed Tropicbirds soaring about when a Pueo, the Hawaiian version of Short-eared Owl, flew before us, doing its wing-clapping display, snapping its wings together below its body."

BOB SUNDSTROM is a skilled birder with a special interest in bird song. Since 1989, he has led Victor Emanuel Nature Tours to Hawaii, Mexico, Belize, Trinidad and Tobago, Iceland, Antarctica, Papua New Guinea and the Southwest Pacific, and many destinations throughout North America. Bob also leads a program of short, regional tours that begin in the Seattle area. He holds a doctorate in anthropology from the University of Washington, and maintains an avid interest in both the natural and cultural settings of his tours. During two seasons of natural history work in the Pribilof Islands, Bob helped chronicle the occurrence of North American bird rarities; he is a member of the Washington State Bird Records Committee, and is a coauthor of The National Audubon Society Field Guide to the Pacific Northwest. Bob is the lead writer for the daily public radio program BirdNote, broadcast in the Pacific Northwest. BirdNote is archived at www.birdnote.org. He and his wife, Sally, live in the rural Scatter Creek Valley south of Olympia, Washington.

DESTINATION 21

IF YOU GO

▶ **Getting There:** Some direct flights from Los Angeles and San Francisco to Kauai are available on United and American Airlines; other flights to Kauai go through Honolulu or Maui.

▶ **Best Time to Visit:** The best time to bird Kauai coincides nicely with the best time to depart the northern regions of the United States—January through early April.

▶ **Guides:** A number of tour companies serve Kauai, including Field Guides (800-728-4953; www.fieldguides.com) and Victor Emanuel Nature Tours (800-328-8368; www.ventbirds.com).

▶ **Accommodations:** The Kauai Visitors Association (800-262-1400; www.kauaidiscovery.com) provides a comprehensive listing of accommodations on the "Garden Isle."

HORTOBÁGY NATIONAL PARK

RECOMMENDED BY **János Oláh, Jr.**

The steppe habitat of the Great Hungarian Plain is unique in Europe. Bordered by the Carpathian Mountains to the east and north and the Transdanubian Medium Mountains in the south and west, the Great Hungarian Plain comprises over 20,000 square miles—almost 60 percent of the country. Among the expanses of this vast plain, Hortobágy National Park stands out. "Hortobágy is the only intact grassland in the Carpathian basin," explained János Oláh, Jr.. "As such, it is home to several rare avian species, and attracts many others on their migratory path. Over 330 species have been recorded here. Hortobágy is special for Hungarians, not only for its natural qualities, but from a cultural perspective. Hungarians are renowned as horseback riders, and we've always been associated with animal keeping. Hortobágy is close to our heart because it reminds us of our connection to the land and our ancestors."

Hungary is about as central in central Europe as a nation could be. It shares borders—clockwise—with Slovakia, Ukraine, Romania, Serbia, Croatia, Slovenia, and Austria. Owing in part to its strategic position on the global map, Hungary has had its share of turbulence. Parts of the nation were occupied by Turkey in the sixteenth and seventeenth centuries, representing the Ottoman Empire's farthest push west. By the nineteenth century, the Austrian Hapsburgs had taken control of the nation. Hungary was divvied up by European powers after World War I, then dominated by the Soviets for forty years after World War II. In 1990, Hungary reasserted its independence with free elections.

Hortobágy National Park rests in the eastern section of the Great Hungarian Plain, near the town of Debrecen. The park's 320 square miles of grasslands and ponds are home to herds of gray cattle, Racka sheep, wooly mongolian pigs, and oxen, which are allowed to graze freely. The grazing of these domestic animals' wild forebears in eons past helped these grasslands gain their final form, after the work of the Tisza River was done. (Now receded to more modest proportions,

the Tisza rests at the western edge of the park.) Sometimes the grasslands are referred to as *puszta*; however, János was careful to clarify that in Hungary, the term extends to mean the shepherd culture.

For some travelers, Hortobágy is known for the frequently photographed Kilenclyukú híd (Nine-Holed Bridge) and for its long-armed sweep wells; for birders, there are other attractions. "Many special moments at Hortobágy come during migration times," János continued. "The whole national park becomes a wetland in the spring. The steppe has many little depressions and marshlands, and they all fill in with water after the rains and snowmelt. This habitat is very important for Arctic species." The spring sees vast flocks of geese, sometimes approaching two hundred thousand, visiting the park. Most of these are Greater White-fronted Geese, but Greylags and Bean Geese are frequently seen, with Red-breasted Geese appearing less regularly. Hortobágy is also a significant stopover for the European population of Lesser White-fronted Geese, classified as a threatened species.

In the fall, Hortobágy is the setting for several memorable appearances. Large flocks of Common Cranes (sometimes called Eurasian Cranes) appear in September. The number of cranes visiting Hortobágy has increased dramatically in the last two decades, going from 3,000 to nearly 100,000. "The cranes are the symbol of the park," János said. "Many birders come to see the cranes. There's always been a strong migration through the Carpathians, but many think the increasing numbers are due to a westward shift in their migration routes. The cranes are here for most of the fall, and are concentrated in three or four roosting places."

A favorite Hortobágy visitor for many, including János, is the Dotterel, a member of the plover family. "We have affectionately nicknamed them 'little stupids,' as they're so tame. They breed in Scandinavia, in high, snowy terrain. It's very difficult to find them there. Hortobágy is the place where many European birders will come to see them. They usually arrive in large flocks—50 to 300 birds. There's a spot in the southern part of the park called Angel House where the Dotterels congregate. There's a thatched-roof barn and some sheep grazing, and grassland as far as you can see. You can sit with the Dotterels running around you, with just the sound of the bells of the sheep in the air."

There are two resident species in Hortobágy that are closely associated with Hungary—the Saker Falcon and the Great Bustard. The Saker Falcon, whose image graces the fifty-forint coin, is nearly the size of the Gyrfalcon, and ranges from eastern Europe to Manchuria. Populations have been dwindling, causing the Saker to be categorized as endangered. Some believe that the decline can be credited to illegal capture of the birds for falconry.

OPPOSITE:
A Great Bustard puffs up in courtship display.

Great Bustard males are among the heaviest birds capable of flight in the world, using a more-than-seven-foot wingspan to propel their thirty pounds along. "Great Bustards used to be common all over Europe, but they've become rarer and rarer," János said. "The population is at around 1,400 in Hungary, and seems to be stabilizing. The display of the males, which generally occurs in April, is just incredible. There are several reliable spots to catch them. You have to go into the spot while it's dark and sit in cover, in hopes they'll display in the early morning. If the males show and a female presents herself, all the males will go in one direction. They then take in four or five litres of air—their necks are so puffed up, they can barely see. They look like big white puffy balls against the green grasslands."

JÁNOS OLÁH, JR. started birding when he was a child. He graduated from the University of Debrecen, Department of Ecology, and is continuing his Ph.D. studies in ecology. János speaks and writes perfect English and is learning Spanish. In Hungary, he conducts field ornithological studies on the steppe, with a keen interest in shorebirds. He has published six papers in Shorebird. He is fond of bird photography, publishing pictures in Birding World and several European and Hungarian journals. He has traveled with camera and telescope throughout the world. János is a member of the Hungarian Rarity Committee and is the founder of the Hungarian Birdline. In the last few years he has led tours for foreign visitors on the Hungarian steppe, in the Zemplén Foothills, and in the Carpathians in Slovakia and Transylvania. He is a coauthor of the guidebook Birds of the Hortobágy and an editor of the forthcoming 3-volume guide Birds of the Carpathians.

IF YOU GO

▶ **Getting There:** Budapest, Hungary's capital, is served by most major carriers, including Continental, Delta, and Northwest Airlines. Hortobágy is roughly 120 miles to the east; flights from Budapest are available to Debrecen, which is twenty miles from Hortobágy.

▶ **Best Time to Visit:** Spring is most popular for visiting birders; fall is also a good time to visit.

▶ **Guides:** Saker Tours (+36 6621-0390; www.sakertour.hu), run by János's father, leads tours throughout Hungary, including Hortobágy. Hungarian Birdwatching (+36 70-943-4450; www.hungarianbirdwatching.com) also leads tours.

▶ **Accommodations:** Hortobágy Club Hotel (+36 5236-9020; www.hortobagyhotel.hu) is situated in the park. The city of Debrecen has extensive accommodations.

22

DESTINATION

JÖKULSÁRGLJÚFUR NATIONAL PARK

RECOMMENDED BY **Tim Gallagher**

Birding, like any passionate pastime, is an excellent excuse to accumulate new experiences. Sometimes the experience of place can be as uplifting as the birds one might find there. For Tim Gallagher, Jökulsárgljúfur National Park in northeastern Iceland is such a place. "Jökulsárgljúfur may not be the most fabulous place in Iceland to find a ton of different bird species, but it's a great place to hike and has spectacular scenery," Tim said. "Jökulsárgljúfur also has some of the Icelandic birds that I'm most interested in, such as Gyrfalcons and Merlins, which both nest in the park."

Iceland is nothing if not dramatic, a land of fire and ice, of stark, treeless landscapes and a rich mythical folklore that's quite alive among Icelanders. The fire comes from the island's pronounced geothermal activities, which provide a considerable amount of heat and hot water for Iceland's 300,000-plus residents, and from the island's more than two dozen active earthquakes. The ice comes from glaciers, which have carved many fjords along Iceland's 3,000-mile coastline, and constitute 11 percent of the nation's landmass. Much of Iceland was formed (and is forming) from volcanic flows, which explains some of its rugged topography; the birch trees that once covered one-third of the island were cut to make way for sheep grazing, and for the most part, have not been replaced. (Icelanders have two sayings about trees. One goes "There is a naked woman behind every tree in Iceland." The other is, "If you ever get lost in the Icelandic National Forest, all you have to do is stand up!") As for myths and sagas, it seems that every landmark has a supernatural as well as a natural explanation. "According to legend, Asbyrgi Canyon in Jökulsárgljúfur National Park, a massive, horseshoe-shape canyon, was created when the pagan god Woden's horse stepped there and left an impression in the stone," Tim explained. (Geologists, incidentally, believe that Asbyrgi Canyon was created by two catastrophic flood waves from the Vatnajokull icecap in the south of Iceland.) Most of the population lives on or near the coastline, which is

23

DESTINATION

warmed by the North Atlantic Drift Current, making it far more habitable than Greenland, 180 miles to the west.

There are no birds endemic to Iceland, and only seventy-odd species that breed there. However, more than 370 birds have been recorded—with seabirds and waterfowl making up the majority of the vagrants. European listers will visit Iceland in the hope of picking up North American vagrants; to a lesser extent, North Americans will stop in Iceland to observe birds of Scandinavian lineage. Traveling birders have tended to focus their efforts on the island's coastal regions, and around Lake Mývatn. One of the great attractions on the coast is the Látrabjarg bird cliff, on a peninsula up the coast from Reykjavik. Here, huge colonies of Common Puffins and Thick-billed Murre gather.

Lake Mývatn, which is in the northern part of Iceland approaching Jökulsárgljúfur, is world-renowned for its legions of waterfowl. "Mývatn means 'Midge Lake,'" Tim added, "so you should expect to be covered with tiny midges most of the time you're there. Fortunately, they don't bite." The midges are an excellent food source for larger lake creatures, which in turn nurture all fifteen species of duck found in Europe, including Harlequin Duck and Barrow's Goldeneye. (Anglers will know Lake Mývatn as the headwaters for one of the world's most famous Atlantic Salmon rivers, the Laxa i Adaldal.)

Jökulsárgljúfur National Park rests roughly between Lake Mývatn and the northern coast, about sixty miles east of Husavik, the closest larger town. The park is marked by its pell-mell, otherworldly geologic formations, largely the result of either a volcanic eruption under the bed of the Jökulsá á Fjöllum River 8,000 years ago, or the handiwork of assorted Norse deities. Jökulsárgljúfur includes some of Iceland's most breathtaking national wonders within its boundaries. In the south is the Dettifoss waterfall, considered Europe's most powerful, where the Jökulsá spills a column of water 125 yards wide a height of nearly 50 yards, creating a canyon some have likened to a miniature Grand Canyon. "The cliffs here along the Jökulsá are impressive," Tim continued. "Hiking along the top of the cliffs you see Northern Ravens, Gyrfalcons, Merlins, and a few Snow Buntings. The last time I went there, I found a Merlin nest and a Gyrfalcon nest on the same long hike. I remember watching an adult Gyrfalcon feeding its two downy young on a cliff nest. You can see European Golden Plovers and Rock Ptarmigan—a favorite prey item of the Gyrfalcon—on the nearby grasslands." Other notable park attractions include Hljóðaklettar (Echo Rocks), eroded remains of ancient volcanoes; and Karl og Kerling, two monolithic rock pillars on the river that are believed to be petrified trolls.

Birders visiting Jökulsárgljúfur will want to be sure to linger in Asbyrgi Canyon. "The

OPPOSITE:
Gyrfalcons, the
national bird of
Iceland, nest in
Jökulsárgljúfur
National Park.

23

DESTINATION

canyon is partly wooded with birch, willow, and larch, but of course the trees are always very small in Iceland," Tim continued. "These woods have numerous Common Redpolls and Redwings (a large thrush, somewhat similar to an American Robin), and there are Winter Wrens. One of the cliffs in Asbyrgi Canyon has a colony of Northern Fulmars. The flatlands between Asbyrgi and the sea (just outside the park) are also a great place to bird. Great Skuas nest there, at the river delta. You can also find Jaegers, Redshanks, Dunlin, Snipe, Black-tailed Godwits, Whimbrels, and Red-necked Phalaropes."

Understand that you won't have Asbyrgi to yourself. In addition to other visitors, the canyon is believed to be the capital city of the huldufólk (hidden people), who reside in cracks in steep canyon walls.

TIM GALLAGHER is a lifelong bird fanatic. An award-winning writer and photographer, he is editor in chief of Living Bird, the flagship publication of the renowned Cornell Lab of Ornithology. For many years Tim has traveled to faraway places, from the high Arctic to the tropics, to study and photograph birds and report on research. He is the author of Wild Bird Photography, Parts Unknown: A Naturalist's Journey in Search of Birds and Wild Places, and most recently The Grail Bird. Tim is a coauthor of Birdwatching and Where the Birds Are: The 100 Best Birding Spots in North America.

IF YOU GO

➤ **Getting There:** Iceland Air offers service from several U.S. cities to Reykjavik, and then on to Akureyri, which is roughly ninety miles from Jökulsárgljúfur.

➤ **Best Time to Visit:** Despite its northern location, Iceland has a temperate climate and can be enjoyed year-round; however, late spring and summer are the most popular times to visit.

➤ **Guides:** Field Guides (800-728-4953; www.fieldguides.com) and Wings Birding Tours (888-293-6443; www.wingsbirds.com) offer trips to Iceland that sometimes include Jökulsárgljúfur. Valtours (+354 895-1245; www.valtours.is) is a local birding-tour leader.

➤ **Accommodations:** There are campgrounds in the park, but no lodging. A number of lodging options are available in Husavik, north of the park, and are outlined at the Iceland Tourist Board website (www.icelandtouristboard.com).

THE ANDAMANS

RECOMMENDED BY **Pamela C. Rasmussen, Ph.D.**

In the early 1990s, research for the mammoth *Birds of South Asia: The Ripley Guide* took Pam Rasmussen on a barnstorming tour of India and surrounding areas. "As the scheduling turned out, I went in June—not the time most people choose to go," Pam began. "I had just started working for the Smithsonian, and had a chance to get acquainted with birds I'd be covering in the book. I wanted to see as many habitats as I could. My travels took me all over India—the Himalayas, Darjeeling, Sri Lanka, and the Andaman Islands. I only had a few days budgeted for the Andamans; I'd been told that would be enough, though few formally trained ornithologists had been there at that time. I found it a surprisingly birdy place, and while I wouldn't call the birds tame, I also wouldn't say that they were shy."

The Andamans are an archipelago of roughly two hundred islands in the southeastern waters of the Bay of Bengal. Though administered by India, the Andamans are almost 600 miles from Kolkota; they're only 120 miles west of Myanmar (once known as Burma), and this helps explain the presence of flora and fauna with southeast Asian affinities. There are two main islands in the group: Grand Andaman, which is divided into North, Middle, and South Andaman, and Little Andaman, which rests between Grand Andaman and the Nicobar Island chain to the south. Most of the Andaman Islands are unpopulated and remain a tropical idyll, fringed with palm trees and skirted by white sand beaches. Over 80 percent of the Andamans are still forested, with a combination of giant evergreen, tropical evergreen, littoral, and mangrove forest types.

Given the tendency for isolated islands to develop high levels of speciation, it's not surprising that the Andamans boast some nineteen endemic species. While it's certainly off the beaten path, hard-core listers can make an excellent case for making the trip! The precise number of endemics in the Andamans is still something of a moving target. "More than twice the number of endemics occur in the Andamans than we thought when I visited there in 1993," Pam continued.

"It was initially thought that a number of species had shared distribution with the Nicobars. We've now learned that the ornithological affinities between island groups are less. In my research, I found that one of the birds that was thought to be shared with the Nicobars—the Andaman Hawk Owl—was not actually shared. In addition to the Andaman Hawk Owl, there were nine other species that were found to be endemic. There are also several others that you could make the case for being subspecies."

Nearly 200 species have been recorded thus far in the Andamans. The endemics on this list include Andaman Teal, Andaman Serpent Eagle, Andaman Crake, Andaman Coucal, Andaman Green-Pigeon, Andaman Scops Owl, Andaman Woodpecker, Andaman Wood-Pigeon, Andaman Cuckoo Dove, Andaman Treepie, Andaman Drongo, and the Narcondam Hornbill. The Narcondam Hornbill is restricted to Narcondam, a small volcanic island approximately seventy-five miles east the northern tip of Grand Andaman. With a range of less than three square miles, the Narcondam Hornbill has one of the smallest ranges of any bird species; it's estimated that there are 300 birds in existence, and though this number is small, the population is believed to be stable.

One of the great thrills of birding in an infrequently visited place is the opportunity to contribute to the body of scientific knowledge about the avifauna of that place—and perhaps even discover a species that is new to science. Pam Rasmussen has had the distinction of helping to identify and classify new species several times in her career, though much of her work was conducted in the museum, not the field. "For a long time, the nightjars that live in the Andamans—now called the Andaman Nightjar (*Caprimulgus andamanicus*)—were considered a subspecies of the Large-tailed Nightjar (*Caprimulgus macrurus*), which has a wide geographic distribution. Several years ago, an ornithologist named Paul Holt sent me some recordings he'd made of the nightjars that he encountered in the Andamans. It was quite a different call from the Large-tailed Nightjar's, and I decided to investigate further. I went to the natural history museum in London and inspected all the specimens of nightjars from the Andamans. They were really quite different from the Large-tailed Nightjar. An associate and I were going to write a paper making our argument, but someone else beat us to it. Still, it was very exciting. You get a piece of information that gives you a clue that species might not be related, and it sets you on the road to discovery."

PAMELA C. RASMUSSEN, PH.D., is Michigan State University Museum's assistant curator of mammalogy and ornithology, and assistant professor in MSU's Zoology Department. Her research focuses on the diversity, vocalizations, taxonomy, and conservation of the avifauna of southern Asia. She recently coauthored a two-volume book, *Birds of South Asia: the Ripley Guide*, which was published in 2005 by the Smithsonian Institution, as well as curating "Birds of South Asia: History vs. Mystery" at the MSU Museum and Detroit Zoo. Pam has also worked on systematics, ecology, behavior, and zooarcheology of Patagonian seabirds, and coauthored a review of the Mio-Pliocene avifauna of North Carolina. She is a research associate with the Smithsonian Institution and a scientific associate with the British Natural History Museum. In addition, she serves as associate editor of *The Ibis* and is a member of the American Ornithologists Union (AOU) Committee on Classification and Nomenclature. Dr. Rasmussen's work has been profiled in the international journal *Nature* and *The New Yorker*.

IF YOU GO

▶ **Getting There:** Port Blair, the capital city on the Andamans, is served from Kolkata by Jet Air (+91 22-2-850-5080; www.jetairways.com) and Indian Airlines (866-435-9422; www.indianairlines.in).

▶ **Best Time to Visit:** September to November and February to April.

▶ **Guides:** Sunbird Tours (+44 176-726-2522; www.sunbirdtours.co.uk) stops at the Andamans as part of its southern India tour.

▶ **Accommodations:** There are a number of hotels in Port Blair, including Fortune Resort Bay Island (+91 124-417-1717; www.fortunehotels.in) and Peerless Resort (+91 031-923-3462 ; www.peerlesshotels.com).

DESTINATION 24

BLUE MOUNTAINS AND BEYOND

RECOMMENDED BY **Peter Marra, Ph.D.**

Peter Marra has traveled the Western Hemisphere in an effort to understand the factors that drive the survival of migratory birds. Some places are less inviting than others. But one venue he always enjoys returning to is Jamaica, and the Blue Mountains.

"My first trip to Jamaica was in the winter of 1989/90," Peter began. "We were studying patterns of habitat distribution of wintering American Redstarts and Black-throated Blue Warblers, and that first trip we were mostly trying to find study sites, and explored potential spots all over the island. Jamaica is a very difficult place to do this kind of work, especially the Blue Mountains. You have to be able to catch birds, and then follow individuals once they've been tagged. The habitat in the Blues is very steep. Sometimes a bird would fly from one peak to another, and it might take us two days to hike down and up again in pursuit! As it turns out, most of our long-term research sites are on the southwestern end of the island. But whenever I'm over for more than a few days, I try to get over to the Blues for some recreational birding."

Jamaica—situated ninety miles south of Cuba and a hundred miles west of Haiti in the Caribbean Sea—conjures up conflicting media images for outsiders. Once advertisements beckoned American honeymooners with sumptuous waterfall-fed mountain pools, ideal for a romantic idyll; more recently, newspaper headlines have warned visitors of the startling crime rates in the capital city of Kingston. Current divorce rates may call into question the value of a honeymoon (in Jamaica, or anywhere!), and some Jamaica travel insiders consider the crime problem overhyped. Whatever picture you choose to take away of Jamaica, several things are for certain: Bob Marley and reggae still dominate the musical soundscape; and there are few places where you'll find so many endemic bird species in such a compact area. Jamaica, 146 miles long and 51 miles in breadth at its widest point, has twenty-eight endemic species that birders in the company of a competent guide should be able to check off in toto! Combine this lure with rich habitat

OPPOSITE:
The mangrove swamps along the Black River provide excellent habitat for West Indian Whistling Ducks.

ranging from coastal scrub to tropical forests to mountains that reach nearly 7,500 feet, and one understands why many birders are willing to risk both honeymooners and pickpockets to make the trip . . . though in truth, most of the island's birding is far removed from the cities and the Montego Bay–style resorts.

The Blue Mountain range stretches across eastern Jamaica for twenty-eight miles with an average width of twelve miles. The mountains take their name from the hue given off by the mist that often surrounds the higher peaks. Coffee plantations and forestry interests have chipped away at the vast forests that once blanketed the Blue and adjacent John Crow mountains, though the Jamaican government has attempted to control encroachment with the establishment of the 194,000-acre Blue Mountain and John Crow Mountain National Park. "The protection the land receives is not what you'd see in a national park in the United States," Peter continued, "but there's still a decent amount of unspoiled habitat." Roughly 150 species—both migratory and resident—make the mountains their home. Endemics found here include Blue Mountain Vireo, Jamaican Blackbird, Black-billed Streamertail Hummingbird, and Crested Quail-Dove. The first three are easy to come by; the fourth takes a little effort. "You need to know what the Crested Quail-Dove sounds like if you want to find them," Peter added. "If you do your research, you can find them. The Streamertail Hummingbird is one of my favorite birds on the island. Each time you see one, it's like seeing your first. I say this having seen thousands!"

It's customary for birders (and other hardy souls) visiting the Blue Mountains to make a nocturnal ascent to Blue Mountain Peak, the highest point on Jamaica. "Usually, people hoping to see the sunrise from Blue Mountain Peak will stay at one of the lodges near the trailhead," Pete said. "You'll get up no later than three to make the six-and-a-half-mile hike up the mountain, with a flashlight, and someone who has an idea of where they're going (if it's your first time). If you go later, mist and cloud cover may obscure the views. You work up a sweat going up, but it can be pretty cold at the top of the mountain; in fact, the first time I hiked up, I was as cold as I've ever been. But the sunrise is spectacular, and on a clear day you can even make out Cuba in the distance. On the way back down, once the sun is up, you can look for the Blue Mountain Vireo and a variety of warblers. There are lots of wintering migrants here. The same is true around the coffee plantations just below the trailhead."

The Blue Mountains are a high point for many birders visiting Jamaica, but you'd be doing yourself a disservice to limit yourself to this region. "There are many great places to experience," Peter said. "The Cockpit Country—which consists of karst rock—has fascinating topography, and it's an excellent place to find Ring-tailed Pigeon and two of Jamaica's endemic parrots, the Black-billed and Yellow-billed Parrots. [Twenty-seven of the twenty-eight endemics are found here.] The mangrove swamps around Black River and the Font Hill Nature Reserve are a great place to find West Indian Whistling Ducks, which are often seen standing in trees. And no birder visiting Jamaica should leave without a trip to Marshall's Pen in Mandeville."

Marshall's Pen, a 300-acre nature reserve set in rolling hills in the southwest, is owned and operated by ecologist Ann Sutton. Listers who are looking for Jamaican endemics when they arrive at Marshall's Pen will likely leave sated—Chestnut-bellied Cuckoo, Jamaican Woodpecker, Jamaican Mango, Vervain Hummingbird, Jamaican Becard, Jamaican Tody, Jamaican Oriole, Jamaican Euphonia, Yellow-shouldered Grassquit, and Saffron Finch can all be found here. Ann Sutton and her late husband, Robert, have done a great deal to further conservation efforts in Jamaica; Ann continues to lead tours on the preserve.

PETER MARRA, PH.D., is a research scientist at the Smithsonian's Migratory Bird Center at the National Zoo. Recent projects he's been involved with include the movement of diseases such as avian influenza and West Nile virus, urban ecology, and migration ecology. Peter is the author of more than sixty articles, which have been featured in such prominent publications as *Science*, *Nature*, and PNAS. When he's not chasing birds or giving seminars, Pete loves to cook, fish, and play with his kids. He lives in Takoma Park, Maryland.

IF YOU GO

▶ **Getting There:** Kingston, Jamaica, is served by many carriers, including Air Jamaica, American, and United Airlines.

▶ **Best Time to Visit:** Endemic species are present year-round; migrants are present during winter months. Temperatures are fairly consistent year-round, with May/June and October/November being the wettest months.

▶ **Guides:** A number of companies lead tours to Jamaica, including Amazilia Tours (506-849-5850; www.amaziliatours.com) and Wings Birding Tours (888-293-6443; www.wingsbirds.com).

▶ **Accommodations:** For those hoping to climb to Blue Mountain Peak, options close to the trail include Whitfield Hall (876-927-0986; www.whitfieldhall.com), Wildflower Lodge (876-929-5394), and Pine Grove Mountain Chalets (876-977-8009). Marshall's Pen in Mandeville (876-904-5454) is certainly worth a stop; groups and serious birders should e-mail Ann Sutton at asutton @cwjamaica.com to inquire about tours.

DESTINATION **25**

MASOALA PENINSULA

RECOMMENDED BY **Luke Cole**

It was a moth, not a bird, that first aroused Luke Cole's interest in Madagascar. "I spent time growing up and as a young adult in Kenya," Luke began. "Kenya is a mecca for naturalists of all stripes, especially birders. But from the age of ten, when my dad gave me a mounted specimen of a Urania moth, it was Madagascar that captured my imagination. I was living in Kenya, dreaming of Madagascar, thanks to a moth.

"When I was a boy, Madagascar was a monolithic concept to me. I thought of it as an endless rain forest filled with lemurs and snakes. I didn't realize how large and varied the place was; there are as many different habitats as you find in California, and the island is roughly the size of California and Oregon combined. It took me thirty years to get to Madagascar, and when I got there it was on a birding trip. Of my five weeks on the island on that first trip, I spent a week on the Masoala peninsula, where the rain forest tumbles down to the Antongil Bay."

Geologists believe that Madagascar—the world's fourth-largest island, roughly 250 miles southeast of Mozambique—has been separated from the continent of Africa for 150 million years, plenty of time for specialized ecosystems and many endemic species to evolve. Indeed, three-quarters of the island's flora and fauna are found nowhere else in the world! The island's incredible biodiversity makes it one of the world's top ten conservation priorities—and a must-visit venue for listers. "Relative to some places, Madagascar has a fairly small overall bird list, 250 or so species," Luke continued. "The fact that 120 of these species are endemic is what brings birders here. In fact, there are five whole families of birds endemic to the island. Few people have the ambition to see every bird on earth, but many want to see at least a representative of every family. All are represented on the Masoala peninsula."

The Masoala peninsula stretches south from the northeastern side of the island and is Madagascar's largest protected region. The forests here are flanked by 3,000-foot mountains, and receive an average of more than 150 inches of rain annually; they constitute the largest stretch of uncut rain forest on the island, and the only place where the forest runs uninterrupted from the highlands to the sea. In the areas of virgin forest, there is little undergrowth at ground level, as the forest canopy blocks most sunlight from reaching the forest floor. Thanks to the Walt Disney Company, even the most indifferent naturalist will likely be able to identify Madagascar's signature mammal: the lemur. Many of the twenty-eight species of lemur on the island, including the Red-ruffed Lemur and the Eastern Avahi, can be found on Masoala. For birders, prized sightings here include Helmet- and Bernier's Vanga, Red-breasted Coua, Scaly Ground-roller, and the Velvet Asity. "If you were to show a photograph of one bird from the Masoala, it would have to be the Helmet Vanga," Luke added. "The bird's massive bill—a fluorescent blue—is unforgettable."

For Luke Cole, Masoala has meant a thus-far-quixotic quest for the Madagascar Red Owl. "I enjoy owls a great deal, and have seen every other owl in southern Africa and in Madagascar," Luke said. "Owls in general are birds of mystery and, as the Malagasy say, 'of sorcery.' The Red Owl, as the rarest and most elusive of all southern African owls, holds a particular attraction." The Madagascar Red Owl is a member of the Barn Owl family, and in fact closely resembles common Barn Owls, though it is smaller and sports orange plumage and small black spots. For much of the twentieth century, the Madagascar Red Owl was thought to be extinct. However, it was rediscovered in 1993.

A rare treat for visitors to Masoala's rain forests is the Madagascar Serpent Eagle, another species that was thought to be extinct until biologists from the Peregrine Fund came upon the raptor in 1993. The Madagascar Serpent Eagle feeds primarily on chameleons and occasionally on small mammals; it's not believed to eat snakes. The National Park in Masada was established in part to provide safe habitat for this raptor.

For Luke, neither the Madagascar Red Owl nor the Serpent Eagle appeared, though it wasn't for lack of trying. "In 2003, I spent two weeks on the trail of the owl, both with organized tour groups and my own treks, from 4:30 A.M. to 11 P.M.," he recalled. "The flow of the day was: up well before dawn for a bite to eat, then into the forest/desert/bush for the dawn chorus and morning birds, back to camp around 10 A.M. for a brief rest, then some mid-morning birding around camp before lunch, then a brief rest after lunch before an afternoon walk until dark, then dinner, and then an evening walk for nocturnal species. Even though we didn't always find the birds we were seeking, there was always something to see. Sixty feet up in the canopy, there might be a troop of Red-ruffed Lemurs, very vocal and animated. Meanwhile, at your feet there might be the world's smallest chameleon." (Madagascar is home to half of the world's chameleon species.) "I went back

in 2006 for another five weeks, including a week on the Masoala peninsula. With my guide I walked from village to village along the coast of the peninsula, showing photographs of the Red Owl to local residents in hopes that there had been a recent sighting—to no avail!"

While the owl proved elusive, another winged creature brought Luke great joy and no small degree of closure. "On the most recent trip, my wife and I were walking with a guide along the shoreline, and a Urania moth flew across the trail, right in front of us. I began crying to my wife, 'That's it, that's it!' I watched it for ten seconds before it flew off into the forest. Encountering the moth connected my childhood dream with the reality of Madagascar."

OPPOSITE:
Helmet Vanga are
one of the treasures
of Masoala.

LUKE COLE is the director of the Center on Race, Poverty and The Environment (www.crpe-ej.org), an environmental-justice litigation organization dedicated to helping grassroots groups across the United States attack head-on the disproportionate burden of pollution borne by poor people and people of color. Luke served on the U.S. Environmental Protection Agency's National Environmental Justice Advisory Council (NEJAC) from 1996 through 2000, and has served as a member of the EPA's Title VI Implementation Committee. Luke is the cofounder and editor emeritus of the journal *Race, Poverty and the Environment* and coauthor, with Professor Sheila Foster, of *From the Ground Up: Environmental Racism and the Rise of the Environmental Justice Movement* (NYU Press, 2001). When he's not helping to improve the world, Luke is birding. He has birded extensively throughout the United States and Southern Africa, served as chair of the California Bird Records Committee and as a regional editor of the journal *North American Birds*.

DESTINATION

26

IF YOU GO

➤ **Getting There:** Air Madagascar (+33 892-70-18-19; www.airmadagascar.com) has flights from Paris and Milan to the island; from there, you'll want to fly to Maroantsetra, where tours are available if you're not joining a larger tour group.

➤ **Best Time to Visit:** September through November is the prime time for birders to visit Madagascar. "The birds are nesting and singing, and the weather is terrific," Luke offered.

➤ **Guides:** Many tour companies lead trips to Madagascar. Luke had excellent experiences with Rockjumper (+27 33-394-0225; www.rockjumper.co.za), which operates out of South Africa.

➤ **Accommodations:** The Masoala National Park website (www.Masoala.org) lists accommodations in the region for those not traveling with a group tour.

SCARBOROUGH MARSH

RECOMMENDED BY **Jan Pierson**

There are two settings that Jan Pierson particularly likes in this world—marine environs and the mountains. Scarborough Marsh certainly has one of those bases covered. And it turned out that it fit conveniently into Jan's academic schedule in 1974.

"I was a biology major at Bowdoin College in Brunswick, Maine (just north of Portland). In the spring term of '74, after my fill of cellular biology classes, I noticed there was a class that didn't require microscopes—Ornithology. The class had field trips from January through the spring, and one of the places we visited was Scarborough Marsh. Even then, I knew it was a special place. I love the habitat, the smell, the look, the birds associated with it. It has a nice seasonality—from winter snow and ice to greening up in the spring to gold and russets in the fall. I like getting my feet dirty, and the marsh is perfect for that. Everything about Scarborough works nicely for me."

Scarborough Marsh is located a few miles south of downtown Portland, Maine's, population center. The 3,100-acre estuary (managed by the Maine Department of Inland Fisheries and Wildlife) is the Pine Tree State's largest salt marsh, a blend of tidal marsh, salt creeks, freshwater marsh, and woodlands. European settlers harvested salt hay from the marsh and pastured their livestock here through the early 1900s, while periodically ditching and attempting to drain the wetlands. The marsh escaped proposed plans for a town dump, and in 1957 the state stepped in to begin acquiring the land as a preserve. Now the marsh sustains a small group of human clam diggers, and a large number of birds. Avian visitors include a broad variety of waterfowl, egrets, herons, raptors, and shorebirds—all told, more than 240 species have been observed here. Scarborough is a favorite stopping spot for Glossy Ibis, and also home to two sought-after sparrows—Nelson's Sharp-tailed Sparrow and Saltmarsh Sharp-tailed Sparrow. "Until 1995, there used to be just Sharp-tailed Sparrows," Jan explained. "At that time, they were split into two species, and both are found at Scarborough."

Scarborough Marsh rests near the nexus of a number of fine birding spots along the southern Maine coast, a coastline that's a bit sandier and gentler than the rock-ribbed shoreline many associate with Maine. In fact, most birding days here will involve stops at a number of venues. Jan described some potential stops on a day's itinerary. "If you're up early, you might start at Evergreen Cemetery, in a residential section of Portland. During spring migration, Evergreen will often get a pulse of birds that touch down after their night flight. From Evergreen, you might head to Dyer Point near Two Lights State Park in Cape Elizabeth. It's a great spot to pick up seabirds like jaegers, shearwaters, puffins, and razorbills. We might then pop in at Higgins Beach (near Two Lights), as there are some nesting Least Terns and Piping Plovers. Then we'll head to Scarborough Marsh. If we're doing a Big Day, it's always a good place to pick up Glossy Ibis, rarer herons and egrets (Tricolored Heron, Cattle Egret), Nelson's- and Saltmarsh Sharp-tailed Sparrows, and Peregrine Falcons and other raptors. From there, we might head to Biddeford Pool—a famous birding spot in its own right—for shorebirds, seabirds, and ducks. For a change of pace, we might scoot down to Kennebunk Plains to pick up Grasshopper Sparrows, Upland Sandpipers, and other grassland specialties, plus Prairie Warblers. Oftentimes, we'll aggregate other birders on the way, and we'll have quite a posse by the end of the day."

Andy Warhol once said that everyone in America would eventually have their fifteen minutes of fame. Jan experienced his fifteen minutes—or at least the first minute thereof—with Scarborough Marsh serving as a backdrop. "Back in the early 1980s, the editor of *Yankee* magazine became interested in the concept of a Big Day, and wanted to write a piece on it. He was in touch with me, and we set things up so he could come along on one of the big 'Big Days'—the twenty-four-hour deal. There were six of us altogether, a team of three other local birders, me, my dad, and the editor. We started at midnight. The editor was curious, but really not a birder. If you're not a birder, of course, some of the mechanics of a Big Day are mysterious at best. It can seem like four or five people are running around, calling out bird names for no apparent reason; as a non-birder you may not actually see many (or any!) of the birds. Your visual reference points as an outsider are mostly trees or fields or landscapes in general, and you might come away thinking that birding is either magic or lying. By 10 A.M., with fourteen hours to go, the editor was pretty much wiped out, though he did end up writing the article, which had a 'boy, these birders are wacko, but it's a fun adventure nonetheless' slant.

"Somehow, the article made its way to the *Today* show in New York, and their producers decided that a birding segment was something they wanted to use on the show. Naturally, they

wanted a scenic outdoor setting for the taping, and we decided to do it at Scarborough Marsh. They sent a film crew up to do the segment, and the reporter had me standing in front of the marsh, where she was pitching me softball questions. As we're chatting, a Yellow Rail started calling right behind me. That's an outstanding bird to come upon any time, anywhere, especially in Maine. I was so distracted, I had to stop the interview. 'Excuse me,' I said. 'There's a Yellow Rail calling behind me.' And I walked away from the camera to try to find the bird. They kept the cameras rolling. Though they shot ten or fifteen minutes of video, the piece was edited down to just a minute or so in the end, almost all focused on the Yellow Rail distraction, which I think they found amusing."

OPPOSITE:

A Double-crested
Cornorant cruises
Scarborough Marsh.

JAN PIERSON is a founder and current president of Field Guides Incorporated (www.field guides.com), a company offering more than 125 birding tours annually worldwide. Jan is a veteran of more than thirty years of international birding and has traveled far and wide to all continents, yet his favorite birding experiences remain simple ones: spring warbler migration in Maine, savoring good long looks at birds, be they rare or common, tropical or temperate, and showing birds to others and watching them thrill at their discoveries. Jan and his wife, Liz, co-authored A Birder's Guide to Maine (Down East Books, 1996).

DESTINATION

(27)

IF YOU GO

➤ **Getting There:** Scarborough Marsh is approximately ten miles south of Portland, which is served by many major carriers, including Continental, Delta, and United Airlines.

➤ **Best Time to Visit:** Late spring through early fall are the most popular times to visit Scarborough Marsh.

➤ **Guides:** The Maine Audubon Society (www.maineaudubon.org) provides both guided tours and materials for self-guided tours at Scarborough.

➤ **Accommodations:** Portland offers a taste of urban life; the smaller towns north and south offer countless bed & breakfasts. The Maine Office of Tourism (888-624-6345; www.visit maine.com) has a comprehensive list of lodgings.

MONOMOY NATIONAL WILDLIFE REFUGE

RECOMMENDED BY **Wayne R. Petersen**

D E S T I N A T I O N

28

Wayne Petersen first wandered the beaches of Monomoy at age thirteen. But it was an event a little earlier that same year—1956—that set him on the path to the Cape, and ultimately a career in birding.

"I can't remember a point in time when I wasn't interested in birding and natural history," Wayne began. "By the time I was in fifth grade, I was hooked. My first personal birding milestone came in seventh grade, when another kid (Richard Forrester) and I discovered an Arctic Three-toed Woodpecker (now known as Black-backed Woodpecker) on a dead elm in our town of Wellesley, Massachusetts. We had virtually memorized T. Gilbert Pearson's *Birds of America*. For whatever reason, the two three-toed woodpeckers in the book were facing each other, one on the left, one on the right. We both looked at each other and said, 'It's the one on the left!' I called the Massachusetts Audubon Society, and the woman on the other end of the phone was very polite, not condescending at all. She put me in touch with some adult birders in town, and they promptly came to confirm our sighting. Somehow, word of this got to Wayne Handley, who was a columnist for the *Boston Herald*. The next Sunday, news of our discovery was mentioned in his column. In the locker room the following Monday, my phys ed teacher said in front of all my peers, 'I understand you found a rare bird, and you're famous.' Now my birding obsession was out in the open, but I felt like a celebrity."

About the same time, Wayne's family began going to Chatham on Cape Cod to visit friends who fortuitously, had a boat. "Their son, who was about my age, was allowed to drive the boat on his own," Wayne recalled, "and he'd take me out to Monomoy and drop me off. I can remember walking the flats, field guide in hand and binoculars around my neck. There were Whimbrels, Red Knots, thousands of shorebirds—my first great memory of Monomoy. When I was in college in the mid-60s, I worked for Massachusetts Audubon at a sanctuary they maintain in Wellfleet. We used to run beach buggy birding tours to Monomoy with 4-wheel-drive flatbed trucks that we rigged up with seats in the back, a wooden canopy top, and canvas sides that could be rolled down as needed. We'd meet the tour groups at Chatham Lighthouse, then ferry them over to Monomoy and load them up on the truck. Those were the golden years, living at the sanctuary with several other guys who were crazy about birds. I think those summers were when Monomoy was galvanized in my mind."

Monomoy National Wildlife Sanctuary is an eight-mile sand spit that extends due south from Chatham, Massachusetts, at the "elbow" of Cape Cod. Monomoy's physical character is ever-shifting. Through the 1800s, it was a series of small islands. By 1900, it was a continuous strip of sand connected to the mainland. In 1958, a spring storm severed Monomoy's connection to the continent. And in 1978, a winter storm cut through the island, creating North and South Monomoy Islands. The one constant at Monomoy is the area's 7,604 acres of spectacular migratory stopover habitat—a patchwork of dunes, tidal flats, freshwater ponds, salt and freshwater marshes—that is used by a great variety of migratory species. In fact, Monomoy was designated a Western Hemisphere Shorebird Reserve Network regional site in 1999. As naturalist Jackie Sones has written on VirtualBirder.com, "If you are interested in shorebirds and terns, North Monomoy Island and South Beach are two of the most exciting places you could visit in the Northeast during the late summer and fall."

During its peak times, Monomoy is indeed a shorebirder's delight. More than forty species of plovers and sandpipers have been observed here, from the common (Sanderling and Semipalmated Plover) to the rare (Eurasian Curlew and Little Stint). Thanks to rejuvenation efforts spearheaded by the U.S. Fish and Wildlife Service's Avian Diversity Program, Common Terns nesting at Monomoy have increased from fewer than 300 pairs in 1996 to over 10,000 ten years later, making it the largest such colony on the eastern seaboard. Populations of Roseate Tern, Piping Plover, American Oystercatcher, and Black Skimmer have also been positively impacted by the recovery program. In addition to breeding terns and oystercatchers, there can be impressive songbird fallouts following autumn cold fronts and northwest winds. "One can sometimes get numbers of flycatchers, thrushes, warblers, and sparrows dropping in," Wayne added, "though most birders can't cash in on these gifts, as it's not easy to get out here before the birds have moved on."

If there's one rare species that hard-core birders associate with autumn migration at Monomoy, it's the Hudsonian Godwit. "These birds have one of the most spectacular migrations of any shorebird," Wayne continued. "After nesting, practically the entire population moves into western James Bay. When they depart in the late summer and early fall, they make a nonstop flight to South America, very seldom touching down on the Atlantic seaboard. If you were to look at schematics of

DESTINATION

28

D E S T I N A T I O N

28

stopovers, they'd show that the Chatham area consistently produces the highest counts on the eastern seaboard. At times, we'll see as many as 150 Hudsonian Godwits at once at Monomoy."

One of Wayne's most vivid recollections of Monomoy dates back to his carefree late sixties summers leading tours for Mass Audubon. "It was early September, and I was going to be leading one of my last tours before heading back to school. It was an absolutely gorgeous, cool day, with a northwesterly wind—which all boded well for the day's birding potential. The day's tour had been chartered by a ladies' garden club from Worcester. When they showed up at Chatham Lighthouse, they were nicely dressed, right down to their proper shoes with block heels. Though obviously not birders in the traditional sense, they were nonetheless very enthusiastic—though I must say that if I were to pick a group of twelve people for what promised to be a banner day, they wouldn't have been my A-team.

"As we approached Monomoy, there were tons of birds around—I could tell that my pre-monitions had been correct. I got everyone loaded into the truck, and we started on our way. It was unequivocally the best single day I've ever had at Monomoy—115 species. And this was with little support from the rest of the group. The ladies were delightful throughout, though they couldn't have cared less about all of these birds. It was just a nice outing at the beach for them. I seem to recall that the highlight for the garden club came at the end of the day, when a Red-breasted Nuthatch landed on my hat. They were all very tickled by this.

"Even now, forty years later, I can't help but wonder what I might have been able to find that day in September had I had a few serious birders along."

WAYNE R. PETERSEN is director of the Massachusetts Important Bird Areas (IBA) Program at the Massachusetts Audubon Society. He was the senior Field Ornithologist at Mass Audubon for fifteen years before assuming the position of IBA director in 2005. As coauthor of Birds of Massachusetts (1993) and coeditor of the Massachusetts Breeding Bird Atlas (2003), Wayne's knowledge of the habitats, distribution, and status of the Commonwealth's bird life is both extensive and wide-ranging. A New England regional editor for North American Birds magazine and editor of the New England Christmas Bird Count, Wayne's knowledge of the seasonal distribution of New England bird life gives him a wide perspective when thinking about important bird areas in Massachusetts and beyond. He currently chairs the Massachusetts Avian Records Committee (MARC) and is an associate member of the Massachusetts Natural Heritage and Endangered Species Advisory Committee.

IF YOU GO

➤ **Getting There:** Monomoy is on Cape Cod, roughly two hours from Boston and Providence, Rhode Island. To reach Monomoy, you'll need to take a short boat ride. Shuttle service is provided by the Monomoy Island Ferry (508-945-5450; www.monomoyislandferry.com) and Outermost Harbor Marine (508-945-2030; www.outermostharbor.com).

➤ **Best Time to Visit:** Spring tends to be best for migratory birds, and late summer is best for shorebirds. If storms arise in September, rare vagrants might appear.

➤ **Guides:** Tours of both North Monomoy and South Beach are offered by the Massachusetts Audubon Society's Wellfleet Bay Wildlife Sanctuary (508-349-2615; www.wellfleetbay.org).

➤ **Accommodations:** The Chatham Chamber of Commerce (800-715-5567; www.chatham capecod.org) provides a comprehensive list of area lodgings.

DESTINATION

28

EL TRIUNFO BIOSPHERE RESERVE

RECOMMENDED BY **Mark Willuhn**

In many of life's endeavors, the path to the goal is as significant as the goal itself. This can be said of the adventure that awaits those who visit El Triunfo Biosphere Reserve.

"For me, the trip to El Triunfo is both spiritually and physically cleansing," said Mark Willuhn, who helped coordinate a trip to El Triunfo for the Nature Conservancy in 1993 and has been back many times since. "It's an active hiking itinerary, but you don't have to be a super athlete. From the wonderful *campesino* cuisine and culture to the spectacular sense of place one gets in the cloud forest to the exhilarating exercise, my trips to El Triunfo leave me ready to take on the world again. There are so few places left where biodiversity is so strong it seems to ooze out of everything. El Triunfo is such a place."

El Triunfo is a 300,000-acre reserve that rests in the Sierra Madre mountains of southern Chiapas. The lower elevation regions of the reserve are a mosaic of tropical lowland forest from dry to remnant evergreen forests, the upper reaches (which have elevations exceeding 7,500 feet) comprise one of the most pristine and biologically diverse cloud forests in Mesoamerica. The cloud forests at El Triunfo are made up of evergreen trees and giant ferns that rise from dense forest floor vegetation; in some places, branches may be festooned with hanging orchids. They are not perpetually cloaked in clouds, though mist will tend to appear most afternoons. "Being in the cloud forest is like walking in a dreamscape," Mark continued. "You can't necessarily see more than four or five feet. You come to a point when you're walking in this all-white world and feel you're isolated, though you're with a group. You might get this experience in other cloud forests, but on the western slope of El Triunfo, it's especially surreal."

The cloud forest habitat at El Triunfo, combined with its geographical position between the Neoarctic and neotropical biogeographical regions, has made it a rich haven for fauna of all types. Spider Monkey, tapir, Red Brocket Deer, and Tayra (a Mesoamerican member of the weasel fam-

DESTINATION

29

OPPOSITE:
The cloud forests of
El Triunfo have a
dream-like quality.

ily) are regularly observed; signs of jaguar and other cat species are often seen, though sightings of the big cats are rare. There are over sixty species of reptiles, 1500 species of butterflies during peak migration, and somewhere in the vicinity of 400 avian species, including Horned Guan, Resplendent Quetzal, Long-tailed Manikin, Orange-billed Nightingale Thrush, a host of motmots, and the Azure-rumped Tanager, one of the rarest members of the tanager family.

El Triunfo has been carefully managed to both protect its biodiversity and generate income for the local communities through ecotourism initiatives. A nonprofit entity, EcoBiosfera El Triunfo S.C., oversees El Triunfo's ecotourism program, and limits the number of visitors to the reserve at a given time. Birding trips, though hosted by different companies, follow an itinerary similar to the one Mark shares here.

"It's quite an adventure to get there. You drive south on paved roads from Tuxtla Gutierrez to a dirt road that leads in the direction of El Triunfo. From here, you get in the back of a coffee truck (coffee beans are an important crop here) or a 4-WD vehicle and ride several hours to Finca Prussia, a little settlement where the road ends. Now the hike begins. You start in shade-coffee plants, and make your way up 2,500 feet through pine and oak forests that transition into cloud forest and the main camp for El Triunfo. While it's a good elevation gain, it comes over nine miles, and a well-maintained trail with lots of switchbacks makes it manageable. Plus, there are burros to carry your gear. The base camp is in an open meadow, surrounded by thick cloud forest. The first time I hiked into the camp was at night, and I was blown away at the brightness of the stars. I've never seen stars that seemed so close. The camp itself is very comfortable, with a little dorm structure and hot water. The thing guests enjoy most is the interaction with the cooks and park rangers, who've lived around here all of their lives.

"Generally, we're at this camp three or four nights. There's a great trail system from the camp, all in the cloud forest environment—from as short as one kilometer to eighteen kilometers. Visitors have an excellent chance of seeing Horned Guan and Resplendent Quetzals here. For the next phase of the trek, we hike over the Continental Divide; on a clear day, you can see the Pacific. There's cloud-forest habitat, then cypress-dominated forest as we descend to a more primitive camp at Canada Honda. This hike is probably our best chance to come upon an Azure-rumped Tanager. It's also the best jaguar habitat. The next day, we move through middle/lower montane tropical forest to our camp at Limonar. This is where we'll generally see motmots. Sometimes there will be many hummingbirds and warblers, too. The last day on the trail brings us down to La Encrucijada Biosphere Reserve on the Pacific Coast. We take a boat to a research station on the preserve, and spend a few nights there, on the banks of the Huixtla River. You wiggle your toes in the mud along the shoreline. When you feel something, you wiggle it up—and it's a pottery shard from the pre-Classic Mayan era from Zoque culture.

"In the course of a week at El Triunfo, you see an entire watershed, cross the Continental Divide, and see some very special animals. It's really a spectacular thing."

MARK WILLUHN is the founder of Emerald Planet (www.emeraldplanet.com), which designs, plans, and carries out conservation-based tours with the goal of generating revenue for protected areas and conservation organizations. He has fifteen years' conservation experience, including extensive work developing sustainable tourism programs and leading tours in Southern Mexico, Belize, Honduras, Guatemala, Nicaragua, and El Salvador. Currently, Mark manages the Mesoamerican Ecotourism Alliance, an innovative business model that builds local capacity; links small-scale ecotourism programs to local, regional, and international markets; and maximizes conservation benefits to protected areas in the region. Before founding Emerald Planet in 1995, Mark held positions as trips coordinator/development associate with the Nature Conservancy, and advancement officer with the Sierra Club. He has guest lectured at the graduate level at Colorado State University and the University of Colorado, participated and presented at numerous workshops relating to microenterprise development, resource development and sustainable tourism. Mark is affiliated with the Center for Protected Areas Management and Training at Colorado State University. He holds an undergraduate degree in forestry from Colorado State University and an M.B.A. from San Francisco State University.

DESTINATION 29

IF YOU GO

▶ **Getting There:** Trips to El Triunfo begin at the Chiapas city of Tuxtla Gutierrez, which is served via Mexico City by Mexicana Airlines.

▶ **Best Time to Visit:** January through April are most popular, with mid-to-late March being the best time to see Resplendent Quetzals while migrants are still present.

▶ **Guides/Accommodations:** You'll need to travel with a tour company to visit El Triunfo, as access is limited to protect this biosphere. MesoAmerican Travel Alliance (800-682-0584; www.travelwithmea.org) leads trips to the region; Victor Emanuel Nature Tours (800-328-8368; www.ventbirds.com) pioneered birding excursions to El Triunfo.

CAPE MAY

RECOMMENDED BY **Luke Dempsey**

There are big days, and then there are BIG DAYS. As far as America's competitively oriented bird-ers are concerned, the World Series of Birding—held each May in Cape May, New Jersey—is the biggest of big days. It brings together some of the world's most celebrated birders—and some who are simply passionate about their pastime. Luke Dempsey would probably place himself in the latter category.

"I first went to the World Series in 2003, with my birding buddies Don and Donna," Luke began. "We've never officially entered, though we never miss a World Series weekend. The three of us are not really big listers. While everyone has a bit of that in them, we're most interested in simply looking at birds."

Cape May was not a completely random choice for the World Series of Birding. Jutting off the southern tip of New Jersey into Delaware Bay and the Atlantic, the region is ideally situated along the Atlantic Flyway to provide a resting spot for migrating songbirds—especially if condi-tions conspire to create a fallout. "After flying over Chesapeake Bay, the birds see green, and if they're tired, they fall in," Luke explained. "The habitat is extraordinary. There are ponds, dense woods, marshes, tidal flats, and beach. The people at the Cape May Observatory—led by Pete Dunne and New Jersey Audubon—do a wonderful job maintaining the preserves and providing guidance for visiting birders." Long before modern birding heroes wandered Cape May—the Meadows (officially known as Cape May Migratory Bird Refuge), Higbees Beach, The Beanery, Cape May Point, Stone Harbor Point—their forebears were here: Records indicate that Alexander Wilson conducted studies here with George Ord as early as 1808. Their work here led to the nam-ing of the Cape May Warbler, as well as the plover that bears Wilson's name.

"Cape May is undoubtedly one of the most heavily birded spots in America," Luke contin-ued. "Little if anything is ever missed; if there's a rare bird there, it will be seen! One World Series

OPPOSITE:
Since the early 1800s
Cape May has
attracted birders,
and the numbers
reach critical mass
during the World
Series of Birding,
held each May.

135

Weekend there was a report that a Purple Gallinule (seldom seen as far north as New Jersey) was hanging out at the Wetlands Institute parking lot. We saw it simply by going where the droves of other birders were. Sometimes I wonder if some of Cape May's notoriety for rarities is a result of what some call the 'Patagonia Rest Stop Theory.' Years ago, a bunch of good birders were sitting at a rest area in southern Arizona, and they saw a number of rare birds. Did this mean that the rest area was a great place for birds, or that these four guys were very good birders? Certainly many of the country's best birders are drawn here, World Series Weekend or not."

But during World Series Weekend, they're definitely here!

The World Series of Birding was born in 1984, when thirteen teams sallied forth to see how many birds they could find in a twenty-four-hour period. The objective—other than some good fun—was to raise money for some conservation organizations and raise awareness regarding the habitat needs of migrating birds. That first competition was won by a team led by none other than Roger Tory Peterson, which tallied 201 species. Since that first event, the World Series (which is sponsored by the New Jersey Audubon Society) has grown to include nearly a hundred teams competing in four categories. Teams raise money by getting pledges for the number of birds they find; to date, more than $8,000,000 has been raised for conservation efforts; team members can give their funds to the organization of their choice. The 2006 event was won by Team Sapsucker from the Cornell Lab of Ornithology, cocaptained by lab director John Fitzpatrick. (While Cape May is the official site for proceedings, teams can wander throughout the state of New Jersey, or even compete in various "limited geographical area" contests . . . though considering that more than 400 species have been identified around Cape May—and that the biggest big day yielded 229 species—why someone would want to go elsewhere is difficult to say!)

"On World Series Weekend, you can't move around Cape May, for all the birders," Luke offered. "Every bird a team identifies is logged. I suppose that one reason we don't compete is that we don't want to be secretive. If I see a beautiful bird, I want to share it with other folks."

It's not all Big Days and songbirds at Cape May. One of the year's most exciting occurrences is the fall raptor migration, which is carefully chronicled by HawkWatch, a group of birders that stakes out a platform in Cape May State Park to observe the procession. "If you show up on a weekend in October or November, you stand on the platform with the HawkWatchers," Luke described. "A docent will shout out what hawks are flying by and where they are. You might see thousands of hawks in the course of a day, and the HawkWatchers keep a running tab. [In 2006, 48,617 hawks were recorded.]

"On one fall trip, we found ourselves at Higbees Beach around 3:30. We went to one of the viewing platforms at the edge of the woods, and waited. Hawks tend to stop their day's migrating late afternoon. We watched in awe as hundreds of Cooper's and Sharp-shinned hawks flew into the trees around us to roost. I still go cold thinking about it. They continued flying in until 4:10; we didn't see another bird after 4:15. It was a great magical moment, one I list among my best birding experiences. I think it could only happen at Cape May."

Luke Dempsey is editor-in-chief of Hudson Street Press, an imprint of Penguin Books, and is also writing a comic birding memoir A *Supremely Bad Idea*, for Bloomsbury.

IF YOU GO

➤ **Getting There:** Cape May is about forty-five minutes from Atlantic City (served by Delta) and one hour and forty-five minutes from Philadelphia (served by most major carriers).
➤ **Best Time to Visit:** The World Series of Birding occurs each May around Cape May, coinciding with the presence of many migrants. October and November are prime time for the raptor migration.
➤ **Guides:** The Cape May Birding Observatory (609-861-0700; www.njaudubon.org/Calendar/Cal CMBO.html) leads outings throughout the year.
➤ **Accommodations:** The New Jersey Audubon Society (609-884-2736; www.njaudubon.org) has assembled a list of accommodations around Cape May.

BOSQUE DEL APACHE

RECOMMENDED BY **Arthur Morris**

Magical. Spiritual. Inspirational. These are the descriptives most often applied to Bosque del Apache, a sanctuary of special enchantment in "The Land of Enchantment."

"My first visit to Bosque del Apache was in December of 1993," Arthur Morris began. "My late wife, Elaine, and I had made a cross-country trip by motor home as part of a sabbatical from our teaching jobs in New York City. After visiting my mother in San Diego, we started east, and decided to stop at Bosque. We came to a spot where you could drive down to some fields, and we came upon what must have been at least 60,000 Snow Geese carpeting the equivalent of twenty football fields. Looking up, we saw a Bald Eagle flying in from the north. This initiated an amazing blast-off, beginning a half mile to the north, with the birds moving in a southerly direction like a tidal wave, fleeing from the eagle. Both Elaine and I stood there with our mouths hanging open. The weather forecast for the next day said snow, so we figured we had better get going.

"We made another western trip that spring, but didn't make it to Bosque. Upon our return home from that second trip, Elaine was diagnosed with cancer. She died on November 20, 1994. Soon after, I returned to Bosque to lead a photography workshop. It began the long, slow process of healing. That year—just two weeks after Elaine's death—I made two images that were later awarded prizes in the Wildlife Photographer of the Year competition. One even made the wrap-around cover of a book that featured the best images from twenty years of the contest. I've now been back twelve years in a row at Thanksgiving time, paying homage to Elaine's memory."

Bosque del Apache is a 57,000-acre refuge that adjoins twelve miles of the Rio Grande River in south-central New Mexico, just south of the small town of San Antonio. Situated on the northern edge of the Chihuahan desert, Bosque has a mix of riparian and arid upland habitat, with mesas rising to the Chupadera Mountains in the west and the San Pascual Mountains in the east. Though the region attracts a variety of avian life, it is best known as a wintering ground for the

DESTINATION

31

OPPOSITE:
Bosque del Apache is
a magnet for
migrating waterfowl.

geese, ducks, and Sandhill Cranes that congregate along the flood plain after making their way south down the Central Flyway. The area was given its name—translated as Woods of the Apache—from Spanish explorers, who often encountered Pueblo Indians along the river here as they made their way to and fro from Mexico City to Santa Fe along the Camino Real (Royal Road), which bifurcated the grounds where the refuge now stands.

The Bosque del Apache National Wildlife Preserve was established in 1939. Since that time, the U.S. Fish and Wildlife Service, local farmers, and local environmental groups (led by Friends of the Bosque del Apache) have worked together to reinvigorate a landscape that had been compromised by overgrazing, river diversion, and other impacts of human settlement. An extensive series of water impoundments were built, re-creating the wetlands setting that existed before irrigation. Farmers planted corn for the wintering birds to feed upon. And salt cedar (an introduced tree) is being removed and replaced with native cottonwoods. These efforts have paid off— wintering Sandhill Crane populations, which had reached a low point of just seventeen birds at the time of the refuge's designation, have proliferated to numbers approaching 15,000.

Three hundred seventy-seven species of birds have been identified at Bosque del Apache since counting began in 1940. Year-round residents include Greater Roadrunners, a pleasant curiosity for birders hailing from outside the Southwest. In spring and fall, visitors will come upon warblers, flycatchers, and shorebirds, passing north or south. But it's the cranes and geese that bring birders and photographers en masse to Bosque in late fall and winter. Experiencing the dawn fly-out or dusk fly-in of the cranes and geese is one of North American birding's great moments, rivaled by the explosion of thousands of Snow Geese (which the locals call "puffs") that can occur when the birds are startled by predators at any time of the day. A twelve-mile road through the preserve offers excellent access, and the birds, fairly accustomed to human onlookers, allow visitors easy proximity. The Festival of the Cranes, held in November since 1988, is a wonderful time to visit, both for the birds, the fellowship, and a plethora of bird and conservation-oriented workshops, lectures, and artistic displays and performances.

The red-rock mountains and brilliant blue skies of New Mexico leave lay people enthralled. For photographers, the beauty of Bosque rests in its light. "The light is just incredible," Arthur continued. "You can have five or ten totally different lighting conditions in an hour, especially around dawn. The one downside is that you'll have a lot of clear skies, which are not ideal for photography. When I'm heading out there, friends say, 'I hope the weather is great.' I reply 'No, I hope it stinks!' I joke that in all the times I've been there, I've only seen twelve drops of rain.

"On the tenth anniversary of Elaine's death, there was snow on the ground. I was supposed to fly back home, but instead drove down to the refuge. There were thousands of geese and cranes frolicking in the snow; I was like a kid in a candy store, running around and taking pictures. The irony of the situation was, however, not lost on me: Elaine and I had run from the snow on our first visit and now I reveled in it."

ARTHUR MORRIS is a freelance nature photographer and writer specializing in birds. Before turning his talents full-time to photography, he taught elementary school in New York City for twenty-three years. With more than 20,000 of his stunning images published in books, magazines, and calendars all over the globe, Arthur Morris is widely recognized as the world's premier bird photographer. His images are noted for both their artistic design and their technical excellence. His fitting credit line: BIRDS AS ART. His book The Art of Bird Photography is the classic how-to work on the subject. The all-new follow-up, The Art of Bird Photography II, was released on CD only in late 2006. More than 140 photo-illustrated articles by and about him have appeared in print. He is a contributing editor with Nature Photographer and is a Popular Photography columnist. Arthur has been a Canon contract photographer for the past nine years. He was recently named a Fellow by the North American Nature Photographers Association. He has conducted more than 350 slide programs and seminars in the past eighteen years. He currently travels, photographs, teaches, and speaks his way across North America and the world while leading more than a dozen of BIRDS AS ART/Instructional Photo-Tours, Photo-Cruises, and Photo Safaris each year. You can learn more about Arthur Morris at www.birdsasart.com.

IF YOU GO

➤ **Getting There:** Bosque del Apache is approximately ninety miles south of Albuquerque, near the town of Socorro. Albuquerque is served by most major carriers.

➤ **Best Time to Visit:** Most birders will visit in the late fall and winter, when Sandhill Cranes, Snow Geese, Bald Eagles, and ducks are at their highest concentration. Many gather here in mid-November for the annual Festival of the Cranes.

➤ **Guides:** The Friends of the Bosque del Apache National Wildlife Refuge (505-835-1828; www.friendsofthebosque.org) provide extensive resources for self-guided tours.

➤ **Accommodations:** The Socorro County Chamber of Commerce (505-835-0424; www.socorro-nm.com) lists lodging options in greater Socorro.

CENTRAL PARK

RECOMMENDED BY **Lloyd Spitalnik**

"At one point in time, my wife and I traveled the country, hoping to get our 700 North American birds," Lloyd Spitalnik ventured. "We did that; then we wanted to get 700 birds in the lower forty-eight. When we were doing lots of traveling, people would say, 'You're such avid birders. Why do you live in New York City?' My response was, 'Because we have phenomenal birding right in Central Park.' Though there was a time when we traveled almost every month on a birding adventure, we'd never go away in May, because we wanted to be here. If you haven't experienced it, it's hard to believe just how good the birding can be."

Mention of Central Park conjures many images to mind—muggers lurking in the shadows, sprawling rock concerts, gangs of marauding teenagers, depending on your age of reckoning. But birds and bird watchers? It's actually not that much of a stretch. New York City is along the Atlantic Flyway, and when you consider how the greenery of the park's 843 acres must stand out against the city's hundreds of square miles of asphalt and concrete, it makes sense that migrants might stop here, and that some birds might even call the park home. (One of the most famous avian residents of the last two decades has been Pale Male, a Red-tailed Hawk that built a nest on the ledge of a Fifth Avenue apartment building across from the park. When the building's co-op board "evicted" the hawk by removing its nest, public outroar—spearheaded by Mary Tyler Moore, one of the building's residents—reinstated the nest.)

Central Park is not America's largest urban park, but it is the busiest, with over 25,000,000 annual visitors. It is the crowning achievement of famed landscape architect Frederick Law Olmstead and his associate on the project, Calvert Vaux. The park was championed by prominent citizens as an effort to put Gotham on par with Europe's great cities, and to provide more wholesome "nonsaloon" entertainment for working people on their day off. It took twenty years to complete and is celebrated for its "naturalness," though nearly all the park's features are man-made.

OPPOSITE:

Blackburnian Warblers are regular visitors to Central Park.

DESTINATION

32

Over its 130 years of existence, Central Park has had periods of neglect and renewal; today, most New Yorkers recognize it for the oasis it is, and treat it accordingly. (It should also be noted that crime statistics are at an all-time low, with only a hundred criminal acts reported in 2005; this makes Central Park one of the safest urban parks in the world.)

Of Central Park's birding haunts, none is so popular, nor so well chronicled, as the Ramble. The Ramble's thirty-eight acres include many thickets, a man-made stream (the Gill), a pond (Azalea Pond), a variety of trees and plants (originally conceived to show the flora of the Appalachian and Adirondack Mountains), and portions of the lake. Many generations of birders have combed the Ramble, and they've left colorful sobriquets for favorite spots—the Oven, Bank Rock Bay, and the Riviera, to mention a few. High season at the Ramble comes in May, with the arrival of migrating warblers and other neotropic songbirds. "On a given Saturday or Sunday in the middle of May, you might see 200 birders walking the Ramble," Lloyd continued. "On an average day at this time of year, I'll see twenty species of warblers, plus tanagers and orioles. On a good day, I'll see a hundred species. What's interesting to me, though, is not how many birds there are, but how friendly they are. You don't have to worry about being especially stealthy in Central Park. I think it's because the birds must get acclimatized to having so many people around. I've never experienced it anywhere else. When you see my photographs, it's evident that the birds are coming to me."

There are always surprises waiting for birders in Central Park. Movie stars like Kim Basinger might come strolling by (this happened to Lloyd one day); and you might come upon a truly exotic visitor—like a Boreal Owl. "There's something magical about owls," Lloyd continued, "and it was especially exciting to have a Boreal Owl in the park [they very seldom leave the boreal forests of the deep north, and there was only one previous sighting on record for the metropolitan area]. It was in December 2004, and the owl had staked out a spot near Tavern on the Green. Even though it was bitterly cold—around twelve degrees—a few friends and I went every day to stand watch, just to make sure no one harassed the bird. About one thousand people came to see it." To underscore the significance of this event among Manhattanites, the Boreal Owl's visit merited a mention on Vanity Fair contributing editor James Wolcott's blog: "Was it worth getting up in the early morning cold to strap on the trusty Zeisses and stare for more than twenty minutes at an owl? Well, I have to say this bird lived up to his advance billing—compact, finely detailed, imperturbable, wise beyond its years." Incidentally, several New York City birding websites and blogs keep local birders apprised of any curiosities in the park. It's not unheard of for a birder cabbing to a midtown meeting to get an alert on her BlackBerry, causing her to redirect her cab to Central Park West for a quick gander at the species in question!

New Yorkers pride themselves on their ability to get along with each other, despite their many differences. The birding scene is no different. "There are no class, ethnic, or racial barriers to birding in Central Park," Lloyd said. "We have people who are on welfare birding alongside the CEO of a major investment bank. Everyone is treated as an equal. Many international birders from all over the world come through. It's a true United Nations experience."

LLOYD SPITALNIK is a native New Yorker who has birded Central Park for more than twenty years and has seen 220 species in its environs. An accomplished wildlife photographer (www.lloydspitalnikphotos.com), his images have been published in *Natural History*, the *New York Daily News*, several Audubon publications, and a World Wildlife Fund calendar, among others. Lloyd is very active in New York City birding circles; he currently runs a rare-bird alert for the metropolitan area called "Metro Birding Briefs."

IF YOU GO

▶ **Getting There:** Central Park is near the geographic center of the borough of Manhattan, served by subways, buses, and omnipresent taxis.

▶ **Best Time to Visit:** April and May and then September are best for visiting migrants, though avian life is present year-round.

▶ **Guides:** Many excellent resources are available for self-guided birding in Central Park, including Birds of Central Park (www.birdsofcentralpark.com) and the Central Park Conservancy (www.centralparknyc.org).

▶ **Accommodations:** NYC & Company (212-484-1200; www.nycvisit.com) lists thousands of accommodations in the metro region.

DESTINATION

32

JAMAICA BAY WILDLIFE REFUGE

RECOMMENDED BY **Ted Floyd**

Back in 2004, Ted Floyd began an editorial as follows: "I probably shouldn't begin by declaring outright that Jamaica Bay Wildlife Refuge, straddling the border between Brooklyn and Queens, is the best place I've ever gone birding. But I feel comfortable with the following: Jamaica Bay is more fun than anywhere else I've been."

   The Jamaica Bay Wildlife Refuge is easily the most important wildlife refuge in the United States that abuts an international airport (JFK). The refuge—some 9,155 acres of salt marsh, ponds, woodland, island, and open salt water—all rest within the city limits of New York; more specifically, it borders the southern edges of Brooklyn and Queens. (The refuge is part of the larger Gateway National Recreation Area, administered by the National Park Service.) "My first visit there was in September of 1990, on a lark," Ted said. "I took the train from Princeton, New Jersey, up to Penn Station, and then followed a complex series of subway connections. It was a two-hour trip from Penn Station. When I had a car, I would often drive within a mile or two of the place, without ever realizing how close I was. There are no highway signs that read 'Exit here for shorebirds.'"

   It's perhaps fitting that this patch of nature in the shadow of America's densest metropolis is largely a man-made construct. East Pond and West Pond were created under the supervision of master urban planner Robert Moses, in 1951. (One story goes that the ponds were built by the Metropolitan Transit Authority in exchange for Moses's consent for a new subway line to be built to replace a wooden railway near the site that burned down in 1950.) A few years later, trees, shrubs and grasses were planted on refuge lands in an attempt to make the parcel more appealing to birdlife. Trails were also added. With more than 325 species spotted at Jamaica Bay in the last twenty-five years, most visitors would agree that the efforts have been a success.

   The southern shorebird migration is certainly one of the high points of the birding year at Jamaica Bay, reaching its peak late July through August. You're likely to find Greater and Lesser

OPPOSITE:
A Glossy Ibis at West Pond in the Jamaica Bay Wildlife Refuge.

DESTINATION

33

Yellowlegs, Semipalmated Plover, Black-bellied Plover, Common and Forster's Terns, and Semipalmated Sandpiper. Spring and fall bring songbirds and warblers into the refuge; in the fall, they're joined by raptors and profusions of waterfowl. "I think Jamaica Bay is striking in all seasons," Ted continued. "You get regional specialties there, as well as global rarities. You might go out in the summer doldrums when not expecting to find much, and by lunchtime you've seen 110 or 115 species. In winter, great rarities will sometimes show up. As far as I'm concerned, Jamaica Bay is a year-round, all-purpose destination."

The rarities of Jamaica Bay are one of its great attractions to Ted Floyd. Though many of its rarities have two legs, rather than two wings. "It's basically impossible to circumnavigate Jamaica Bay's West Pond without bumping into a 'character'—a wide-eyed tourist or an all-knowing local, a highstrung lister or a laid-back watcher, a cocky kid or a patrician elder," he wrote in 2004. "On a warm autumn weekend, you are likely to encounter dozens. In the dead of winter, you'll cross paths with a few." West Pond has been a gathering spot for passionate five-borough birders since the time it was created. Even before the Jamaica Bay Refuge had its makeover, it shoreline was part of the home turf of such venerable organizations as the Brooklyn Bird Club and the Queens County Bird Club. "Jamaica Bay is a meeting place where all the world's great birders like to go. If they're in Manhattan to give a talk or see their publisher, they'll likely sneak away at some point to Jamaica Bay. It's a place that I would casually pop into when I lived around New York. It's a place that I visit from 2,000 miles away. Its accessibility—both geographically, and in terms of the skill levels that are needed to find some level of success—make it a magnet for birders. On a warm day in the fall, you might see several hundred folks out there—all operating at their own speed."

Jamaica Bay is home to a population of American Woodcocks. Should you visit in the early spring—late March tends to be the most reliable time—male woodcocks may treat you to a showing of their "sky dance." Leaving his hiding spot on the forest floor near dusk, the male will move into an open area (its singing site or breeding field), and begin his call. Then the male will take off, circling higher and higher, making a flittering noise with his wings and chirping loudly in hopes of attracting nearby females for a look. The woodcock's sky dance is made no less dramatic by the sunset backdrop of the Manhattan skyline.

TED FLOYD started birding when he was thirteen years old. The exact date of his conversion was 21 September 1981. After college (A.B. in Biology, Princeton University) and grad school (Ph.D. in Ecology, Penn State University), Ted taught biology at several colleges and universities. Then he migrated into the nonprofit realm, first heading up the *Nevada Breeding Bird Atlas* for the Great

Basin Bird Observatory and now serving as editor of Birding, the flagship publication of the American Birding Association. Ted's major interests are avian status and distribution, bird conservation, and birder education. He also has strong secondary interests in entomology, statistics, and general ecology. Ted has published more than a hundred articles, for popular and professional audiences alike. He is a frequent speaker at birding festivals and ornithological meetings and has led birding trips throughout North America. Ted lives in Boulder, Colorado, with his wife, Kei, daughter, Hannah, and son, Andrew. He has two books on the horizon: The Atlas of the Breeding Birds of Nevada (University of Nevada Press, spring 2008) and Field Guide to the Birds of North America (HarperCollins).

IF YOU GO

➤ **Getting There:** The Jamaica Bay Wildlife Refuge literally abuts the property of the JFK Airport in the borough of Queens.

➤ **Best Time to Visit:** Spring is prime time for songbird and warbler migrants. Fall brings these birds, as well as migrating raptors and shorebirds to Jamaica Bay.

➤ **Guides:** The Gateway National Recreation Area (www.nps.gov/gate) and Brooklyn Bird Club (www.brooklynbirdclub.org) offer excellent references for self-guided birding adventures at Jamaica Bay.

➤ **Accommodations:** NYC & Company (212-484-1200; www.nycvisit.com) list thousands of accommodations in the metro region.

DESTINATION

33

SUB-ANTARCTIC ISLANDS

RECOMMENDED BY **Steve N. G. Howell**

"I'm glad I didn't visit the Sub-Antarctic Islands until later in my career," mused Steve Howell. "If I'd gone as a younger man, I'd have been disinclined to watch seabirds anywhere else!"

New Zealand's Sub-Antarctic Islands dot the Southern Ocean south and east of the South Island of New Zealand. They include the following island groups—The Snares, Bounty, Antipodes, Auckland, and Campbell Islands—all of which lie in the blustery latitudes of the "Roaring Forties" and "Furious Fifties." Macquarie Island is considered part of the group as well, though it falls under Australian administration; The Chatham Islands to the northeast are technically not part of the group, though expeditions spend a few days there before turning west back to the mainland. The islands rest in the middle ground between the Antarctic and Subtropical Convergences, and as such have high levels of biodiversity and endemism. Though exploited by whaling and sealing gangs in the eighteenth and early nineteenth centuries, the Sub-Antarctic Islands are now seldom visited, and largely unblemished. From a birder's perspective, they're remarkable for their seabird populations—considered the most diverse in the world. More than 120 bird species have been recorded here, including multiple species of nesting albatrosses, petrels, and shearwaters. There are also eight species of penguins in the Sub-Antarctic region, and at least fifteen endemic land bird species.

"Nowhere else in Southern Oceania do you have so many islands so close together," Steve continued. "Though they're in the same general area, each island has some different bird speciation—much like the Galápagos. Up to this point, the Sub-Antarctic Islands have not been very well studied. That's appealing to me, as I like going to places that aren't so well known. Making discoveries is part of the fun. If you're really into seabirds, you'll view an expedition to the Sub-Antarctic Islands as the crown jewel of birding."

"Expedition" is not too strong a word for the adventure that awaits the intrepid seabirder

OPPOSITE:
King and Royal Penguins (the smaller species) on Macquarie Island, the sole breeding site for Royals and the most reliable place in the world to find them.

DESTINATION

(34)

151

who sets sail with Heritage Expeditions, the operator licensed to lead trips in this environmentally sensitive region. You're at sea for nineteen days and there are about ten ports of call. At some stops, you'll hike to nesting areas; on other islands, where humans are forbidden to make landfall, you'll cruise the coastline in Zodiacs. Each stop holds special treasures. In his trip notes, Steve underscores some of the high points: "The Snares have millions of Sooty Shearwaters plus Snares Crested Penguins; Enderby Island in the Auckland group is a pristine jewel of restored island biodiversity; Macquarie has millions of Royal Penguins, thousands of Southern Elephant Seals and King Penguins; Campbell is home to the Southern Royal Albatross and flowering megaherbs; the Antipodes have their endemic parakeet and Antipodean [Wandering] Albatross, plus Erect-crested Penguins; the stark Bounty Islands hold almost all the world's Salvin's Albatrosses; and the subtropical Chathams have Shore Plovers, Northern Buller's Albatrosses, and two endemic shags. The relatively short at-sea transits between islands are never dull, with up to ten albatross species accompanying the boat as well as good numbers of many other tubenoses."

On his first trip to the Sub-Antarctic Islands, Steve was fortunate enough to observe one of the rarest seabirds in the world, the Magenta Petrel. "The Magenta Petrel is not magenta in color, but dark brown and white. It takes its name from an Italian ship called *Magenta*. Members of the crew shot the petrel in 1867 off Pitcairn Island in the middle of the subtropical Pacific, and then it sat in a museum for many years, its breeding grounds unknown. Almost a hundred years later, a British ornithologist reasoned that all of the island groups in the Sub-Antarctic region had large species of petrels breeding there, save for the Chathams, and perhaps the enigmatic Magenta Petrel might hail from there. In the 1970s, New Zealand ornithologists spotlighted mystery petrels on the Chathams at night (when the birds visit their nest burrows) and finally caught one—it was a Magenta Petrel! It's believed that there are no more than 150 left in the world.

"The crew of *Spirit of Enderby* (the ship Heritage runs to the Sub-Antarctics) acknowledges there's a slim chance that a passenger might observe the Magenta Petrel, and they offer a bottle of champagne to the lucky finder. I was standing on the bridge one day while people were having breakfast, and I spotted the petrel and screamed it out. I suppose that I nearly deafened the person next to me. Everyone erupted from the galley and ran up on deck. The bird was long gone by then, just a speck in the sky. Miraculously, though, it turned around and flew back right past the ship, giving all comers a view. I took the first known photographs of the bird at sea.

"I joined the expedition the following year, and we took the same route. It was Christmas Day when we passed the area where I'd seen the Magenta Petrel the year before. I stayed outside the whole day, hoping for another look at it. I went up to the deck at dawn and stayed until dark;

people kindly brought me apples and cookies to keep my strength up. There was one bird after another and thirty-one species of tubenoses were seen that day—which is a quarter of the world's true seabird species, including twelve species of albatross (or half of the albatross species in the world!). Life doesn't get any better that that."

STEVE N. G. HOWELL grew up in Cardiff, Wales, where he started birding at an early age, and is now an international bird tour leader for WINGS. It was a trip in 1981 to Mexico—a country where in twelve hours Steve saw 210 species in sunshine (versus 206 species in rainy Wales in twelve years)—that gave him real wanderlust. Since then he's birded around the world, including two years spent at sea. Steve has authored and coauthored a number of books, including *A Guide to the Birds of Mexico and Northern Central America* (1995), *A Bird-finding Guide to Mexico* (1999), and *Hummingbirds of North America: the Photographic Guide* (2002), and over 200 popular and scientific articles. He serves on the editorial board of *Cotinga* (the journal of the Neotropical Bird Club), is book review editor for the journal *Western Birds*, and a research associate at PRBO and at the California Academy of Sciences. With Jon Dunn, Steve recently completed work on a photographic guide to American gulls, and current projects include a photographic identification guide to North American tubenoses, and, with Will Russell and Ian Lewington, a book on rare birds of North America. His "chronic" writing habit was recognized in 2005 when the American Birding Association (ABA) awarded him the Robert Ridgway Award for publications contributing to field ornithology. In recent years, Steve has been an instructor for the ABA's Young Birder Conventions.

IF YOU GO

DESTINATION

34

▶ **Getting There:** Expeditions begin in Dunedin, which is served by Air New Zealand via Auckland. Auckland is served with direct flights from Los Angeles and California by many carriers, including Air New Zealand, Cathay Pacific, Qantas, and Singapore Airlines.

▶ **Best Time to Visit:** Trips are conducted in November and December.

▶ **Guides/Accommodations:** Heritage Expeditions New Zealand, Ltd. (+64 3-365-3500; www.heritage-expeditions.com) is the only outfitter licensed to lead visitors to the Sub-Antarctic Islands Birding companies offering tours in conjunction with Heritage include WINGS Birding Tours (888-293-6443; wingsbirds.com) and Field Guides (800-728-4953; www.fieldguides.com).

GREAT SMOKY MOUNTAINS NATIONAL PARK

RECOMMENDED BY **Alicia Craig**

Great Smoky Mountains National Park is America's most popular national park, seeing upward of 9 million visitors a year. Many come to see one of the park's 1,200 black bears, a symbol of wildness in the increasingly populated southeast. Some—like Alicia Craig—come for the birds.

"I first started visiting the Great Smokies with my parents," Alicia began. "My dad was a teacher, and had the summers to travel. He would point out the plants, trees, and birds; I remember being fascinated with the salamanders. I've been going back on a regular basis for many years. The habitat is incredibly diverse—you go from 800 feet elevation to over 6,600 feet. As the habitats change, so do the birds. Many of the birding spots are easy to get to; you can't go wrong hiking or driving."

Great Smoky Mountains National Park straddles 800 square miles along the border of western North Carolina and southeastern Tennessee. As Alicia noted, one of the park's great attractions for birders is the range of elevations it affords, and the presence of intact old-growth forests. In the highest-altitude areas, you'll find spruce-fir forest. Moving to midlevel elevations, there will be a mix of northern hardwoods and cover hardwoods; here you'll also find a mix of northern and southern bird species. In the southern hardwoods that predominate at lower elevations, one will find the greatest number of species, ranging from Carolina Chickadee and Song Sparrow in the spring to Yellow-billed Cuckoo and Yellow-throated Vireo in the summer and Yellow-rumped Warbler in the winter. All told, 240 species have been identified in Great Smoky Mountains National Park; sixty species are present year-round.

The highest point in the park is Clingmans Dome, which rests at 6,643 feet. There's an observation deck here that offers spectacular 360-degree vistas; on a clear day you can see a hundred miles (though due to increasing air pollution, such clear days are fewer and farther between). "There's a stand of old growth nearby," Alicia continued. "After visiting Clingmans one time, I

DESTINATION

35

OPPOSITE:
*Great Smoky
Mountains
National Park
boasts a tremendous
variety of habitat.*

hiked over there. I heard a Wood Thrush singing in the background, then another. For me, nothing is more beautiful than being surrounded by the old growth in the Smokies and hearing the Wood Thrush, which is in decline, sing. Their song is just magical in those old forests.

"A nice aspect of birding along the trails of a higher-elevation place like the Smokies is that you're able to mitigate the effects of that malady known as 'warbler-neck.' That's because you're often high enough on these mountain trails to look across at the tree-tops, rather than up, to find warblers or whatever else might be up there."

Great Smoky Mountains National Park is crisscrossed with more than 270 miles of roads, giving visitors excellent access to many of the "birdier" regions of the park. There are also many backpacking opportunities for the more adventurous types, and one of Alicia's most compelling memories of her time in the park stems from such a sojourn. "We were on a three-day hike in a lowland section," she recalled, "camped in a very remote area. In the middle of the night, Bard Owls began calling. There were at least four or five of them. It sounded like we were surrounded by monkeys. I found myself laughing out loud, the sound was so hysterical."

One of the more popular drive-in viewing spots for wildlife in general is Cade's Cove, a lush valley surrounded by mountains near the western edge of the park. "There are pull-outs there where you can sit in your car—or walk just a few steps—and observe the valley," Alicia explained. "It's easy birding, and you can see mammal life as well—black bears, white-tailed deer, even red wolf, which have recently been reintroduced to the park. On one occasion some years ago, I was at a pull-out, and had my spotting scope set up, looking out at some edge habitat—a field with woods in back. I was watching two bear cubs and their mother. Several people pulled up in their cars and asked what I was doing. When I said 'bird watching,' they nodded and pulled away. Had they known I was watching bears, there probably would have been a traffic pile-up. One group that stopped was actually curious when I said I was bird watching, and I showed them the bears. I think that today, more drivers would've stopped to look at 'mere' birds. More and more people are interested in birding."

ALICIA CRAIG is the director of Bird Conservation Alliance for American Bird Conservancy. Previously, Alicia worked as a naturalist in Florida and more recently as the education manager and cause-related marketing manager for a national birdfeeding retail chain. She serves on the Association of Field Ornithologists council, the Ornithological Council, and the American Ornithologists Union Committee on Conservation. Alicia also serves on the board of Operation Migration and is the past president of the Amos W. Butler Audubon Society Chapter in

Indianapolis, Indiana. She served as a guest host on the PBS BirdWatch television program series for Connecticut PBS television and as the host for the Wyoming PBS series Backyard Birds. She presents a variety of workshops to organizations and programs for all age groups on bird watching and identification, conservation issues, habitat creation, and Whooping Crane reintroduction.

IF YOU GO

➤ **Getting There:** The western entrance of Great Smoky Mountains National Park (in Gatlinburg) is roughly forty-five miles from Knoxville (served by most major carriers); the eastern entrance (in Cherokee) is sixty miles from Asheville (served by Delta, Northwest, and U.S. Airways).

➤ **Best Time to Visit:** Peak time for migration is mid-April to mid-May in the lower elevations. Species that nest in higher elevations set up house in June.

➤ **Guides:** Victor Emanuel Nature Tours (800-328-8368; www.ventbirds.com) leads trips to the Smokies each spring.

➤ **Accommodations:** The Great Smoky Mountains National Park website (www.nps.gov/grsm) includes links to town chambers of commerce near the park. Leconte Lodge (865-429-5704; www.leconte-lodge.com) is the only lodging in the park, but requires a five to eight-mile hike in.

DESTINATION

(35)

PRAIRIE POTHOLES

RECOMMENDED BY **Julie Zickefoose**

"Central North Dakota is not the first, or even the hundredth, place that springs to mind when most people plan vacations," Julie Zickefoose stated. "It's not flashy or trendy, or even remotely geared to the urbane sophisticate. What it offers is breathtaking beauty, serenity, and a wide-open remoteness that frees the soul. In late spring, it's absolutely alive with breeding birds and animals. They know where to go to be left alone. North Dakota is not on the way to anywhere. It's as much a state of mind as a state, and you've got to want to go there, seek it out, and settle into it, like a meditation."

OPPOSITE:
The "potholes" of the Prairie Potholes were created by the scoring action of glaciers. Some are seasonally filled, others year-round.

The region of North Dakota that Julie references is often referred to as the Prairie Potholes. If you were to draw a triangle between the towns of Carrington, Jamestown, and Steele, you'd capture much of the area, which includes three national wildlife refuges (Chase Lake, Arrowwood, and Long Lake) and assorted sanctuaries/birding hot spots. The term Prairie Potholes references a large swatch of territory stretching from Alberta, Saskatchewan, and Manitoba in Canada to parts of Montana, North Dakota, South Dakota, Nebraska, Minnesota, and Iowa. The land here is characterized by shallow depressions (i.e., potholes) created by the scouring action of glaciers. The potholes collect snowmelt and rain in the spring, providing a breeding ground for a variety of vegetation that in turn draws an abundance of bird life onto these suddenly not-so-lonely plains. It's estimated that the Prairie Potholes across the Upper Midwest host half of North America's migratory waterfowl. Some of the potholes are seasonally flooded; some permanently so, taking on the personality of small marshes or shallow lakes. Almost all of them are productive.

"You stop your car in front of a little pothole, maybe the size of your front yard," Julie continued. "There are eight species of ducks floating around, some trailed by peeping broods of ducklings. Pintail, Blue- and Green-winged Teal, Shoveler, Mallard, Lesser Scaup, Gadwall, and Ruddy Ducks. Or Canvasbacks, Redheads, Ringnecks. Take your choice. Wilson's Phalaropes spin and pick at the water's surface; Black Terns, in colors of cast iron and pewter, dip and dive for minnows. Western- and Eastern Kingbirds sit side by side on a low wire fence. Red-winged and Yellow-headed Blackbirds konk and bray on the fringes. All around, Grasshopper, Vesper, and Savannah Sparrows lisp and buzz. Bobolinks broadcast their shortwave bird radio. You step out of your car to take it all in, and an American Avocet streaks toward you, complaining, as its apricot-fuzzed chicks hurry into the cattails."

For many travelers who find themselves driving across North Dakota at breakneck speed in anticipation of Yellowstone and the Rockies, the less dramatic pleasures of the Prairie Pothole region might go unnoticed. Yet there's much to be appreciated. The tall native grasses wave in the wind beneath a big beginning-to-be-Western sky that's reflected in countless pools of water. The contour of the land is much more nuanced than you might have noticed from Interstate 94. "Every gravel road holds a different geological surprise—high ridges or conical eskers and drumlins—gravel deposits left by the receding ice sheet, now clothed in soil and soft, waving prairie grasses and wildflowers," Julie said. "Unexpected secret gardens hide beneath the grass tops—blue Indian breadroot, cheery gaillardia, purple peas and vetches, scarlet globe mallow, white penstemon and anemone, blue harebell. Best of all, the entire landscape is crammed seemingly past capacity with birds, all hard to see elsewhere, all breeding."

The local chambers of commerce have begun to recognize their feathered citizens' potential for attracting visitors, and have created Birding Drives Dakota—a patchwork of driving routes around the Carrington/Jamestown/Steele triangle. "The roads are perfectly straight, the corners square, so it's hard to get lost," Julie added. "There's nobody else around, so you can crawl along at ten miles per hour, casting your glance across the landscape, and pull over in a heartbeat when a Ferruginous Hawk sails into view. It stays light until 10:30 at night, low, buttery light bathing ducks and shorebirds in gold. And almost every little town has a terrific roadside café, sweetly fragrant with fresh coffee and homemade pies. Could a birder ask for anything more?" The region's celebration of avifuana reaches its apex in early June with the Potholes and Prairies Festival.

Beyond its showier migratory visitors (including the world's largest nesting colony of White Pelicans at Chase Lake), the Prairie Potholes are known for the somewhat less glamorous species—sparrows. Eighteen species are found here, including LeConte's, Nelson's Sharp-tailed, and Baird's Sparrows; these three have a range defined by the upper Midwest. On their first visit to the Potholes, Julie and her writer/editor husband, Bill Thompson, III, had been shut out on the big (little) three until the final day of their stay. And then their luck changed.

"We were on our way to the picnic luncheon that would close the Potholes and Prairie

Festival when we encountered Steve Gross, a delightful, soft-spoken, retired Air Force colonel who was seeking Baird's Sparrow for his North American life list. He'd been told by a local birder that the shortgrass hilltops near the Chase Lake's refuge sign were a good bet. We thanked him and went on. Coming to the third cattle guard, we pulled off and hopped out to listen. A strange sparrow song—soft and musical, with four introductory notes and a slow trill—sifted over the hill. I didn't know what it was, but I knew I'd never heard it before. I took off at a lope through the grass. In the distance, we could see Steve's car, and I saw him focus his binoculars on me. I gave him the thumbs-up and he started walking toward us.

"Single-minded doesn't quite describe us on the quest for a life bird. I was completely oblivious that Prairie Public Television had pulled up in a white van to film Bill and me as we birded. Trailed by Bill, who was carrying the spotting scope and answering rapid-fire questions from an interviewer were a cameraman and a soundman with a large boom microphone, Steve and I headed one, two, three hundred yards into the prairie, without coming much closer to the mystery sparrow's song. Finally it seemed to be singing from underfoot. We strained our eyes into the vegetation, staring into the grass like addled spaniels, wondering if our singer would ever pop up. And it did, a small, streak-breasted, pale sparrow, singing happily, unconcerned about the odd-looking people and equipment focused on it. Over the next hour and a half, it was to circle its territory many times, always fetching up on one small legume that protruded enough from cover so we could observe it. We laughed and whooped softly, and I drew the little bird to my heart's content. The television crew wandered away, and Steve, Bill, and I were alone with the sparrow and the sun and the soft, fragrant air. It just doesn't get any better. And it was all on film!

"Taking fond leave of Steve, we retired to the nearby luncheon. I left my sketchbook open, not too subtly, to a sketch of a Baird's Sparrow, which none of the festival participants had yet found. Soon we had a large charter bus full of excited people hoping to add it to their life lists, too. The heat was on! We led the bus to the spot, found our trail through the grass, and twenty people snaked single-file to the spot where we'd found the bird. And, unbelievably, there it was, singing on its silvery perch, as happy and oblivious to the fuss as it had been three hours earlier. This bird, which may never have seen a human being in its life, now saw two dozen, and every one of them wore a broad smile. Happiest of all was Bill, who loves nothing better than showing new birds to nice people."

JULIE ZICKEFOOSE is a widely published natural-history writer and artist. Educated at Harvard University in biology and art, she worked for six years as a field biologist for the Nature

Conservancy before turning to a freelance art career. She has presented illustrated lectures for nature organizations and festivals across the country, and exhibited her paintings at universities, museums, galleries, and in juried shows. Illustration credits include *The New Yorker, Smithsonian, Spider, Cricket,* and *Ladybug.* She has written and illustrated articles for *Country Journal,* and *Bird Watcher's Digest* has published more than thirty of Julie's articles and seventeen of her cover paintings since 1986. Julie has painted color posters and illustrated educational materials for Cornell University, the U.S. Fish and Wildlife Service, the Smithsonian Migratory Bird Center, and the Boy Scouts of America. Reader's Digest Books, Yale University Press, and National Geographic Books have published her illustrations or writings. The American Ornithologists' Union and the Academy of Natural Sciences employed her as a primary illustrator of their landmark seventeen-volume work, *The Birds of North America.* Julie's writing is a unique personal narrative that creates a mood, yet informs the reader. She accompanies her writing with paintings and drawings. "A South African Tapestry," *Bird Watcher's Digest* (March 1995) took an Apex Award for Feature Writing. Her illustrated book, *The Bird-friendly Backyard: Natural Gardening for Birds* (Rodale, 2001) has sold more than 40,000 copies, and *Enjoying Bluebirds More,* a bluebird landlord's handbook, has sold more than half a million copies. Her most recent book is *Letters from Eden* (Houghton Mifflin); see some of Julie's work at www.juliezickefoose.com.

IF YOU GO

▶ **Getting There:** Most visitors will fly into Fargo, North Dakota (served by Northwest via Minneapolis), and then drive the roughly ninety miles west to the Prairie Potholes region.

▶ **Best Time to Visit:** From May to July, bird diversity and numbers are at their peak. April and October are best for waterfowl migration. Many birders converge here in early June for the Potholes and Prairie Birding Festival.

▶ **Guides:** Birding Drives Dakota (888-821-2473; www.birdingdrives.com) provides extensive do-it-yourself birding information. Dakota Birding (701-845-4762; www.dakotabirding.com) is a locally based guide; Wings Birding Tours (888-293-6443; wingsbirds.com) includes the Prairie Potholes region as part of a regional tour.

▶ **Accommodations:** Birding Drives Dakota (www.birdingdrives.com/lodging.htm) provides an extensive list of lodgings options in the Prairie Potholes region.

Ohio

LAKE ERIE

RECOMMENDED BY **Jim Berry**

The Rock and Roll Hall of Fame and Museum is a stunning I. M. Pei creation that rests on the shores of Lake Erie in Cleveland, Ohio. Since opening its doors in 1995, the Hall of Fame has attracted more than 5,000,000 visitors, drawn to the site to gaze at and listen to pop music's greatest stars.

For birders, the big show—a veritable Woodstock of birding—is scattered along the shoreline of Lake Erie to the west. The curtain goes up in early May when the Neotropical Migrant Tour hits town.

"During the first few weeks of May, thousands of birders are drawn to the southern shore of Lake Erie," Jim Berry began. "This roughly hundred-mile section of shoreline is such an important stopping point for neotropical species migration that there are six identified 'globally important bird areas' in the stretch from Cleveland to Toledo. Some people will spend a day, others will spend a week, hitting a series of parks and reserves along the waterfront. Birders with a modest amount of experience will hardly ever come away with less than a hundred species. Some might hit 200, given a few days in the field. I still fondly remember my first birding experience on the southern shore. It was 1970, and I was enrolled in a beginning ornithology class at Ohio State University. On the way up there, I had noticed in my *Peterson Field Guide* that there were thirty species of eastern warblers that could potentially be seen. That first trip, I saw twenty-six! I've been there that same weekend thirty-three of the last thirty-five years."

Some of America's great fall-out birding locations—Cape May, New Jersey, and High Island, Texas, come to mind—have become concentration spots because migrants have passed over large areas of water, and thanks to wind/weather conditions are unwilling/unable to fly any farther. The phenomenon along Lake Erie is somewhat the opposite, as Jim explained. "The birds that come through here are primarily nighttime migrants. They prefer to start across the lake when they're

rested and have an entire evening ahead. They've just flown across Ohio, which is mostly agricultural land. When they get near the lake, there's a ribbon of woodland—all the parks/preserved
areas are almost interconnected—interspersed with wetlands and lots of cover and vegetation. It's
a natural place for them to stop and wait for the right wind and weather to push across.
Oftentimes, they'll stay for days to feed and rest. Along the lake, you'll see birds from all the different groups—flycatchers, warblers, vireos, thrushes, waterfowl, shorebirds, wading birds, raptors.
There are many Bald Eagles now; where there were just a few nesting pairs left in 1970, you'll see
them almost anywhere on the southern shore today."

Scattered through Erie, Lorain, and Ottawa counties, there are more than thirty birding
spots identified by Lake Erie Wing Watch, a birding interest group. Some of the most highly recommended spots include Cedar Point, Lakeshore Metropark, Magee Marsh Wildlife Area,
Maumee Bay State Park, Metzger Marsh, and Ottawa National Wildlife Refuge. Among these,
Magee may be the most prominent. It offers over 2,000 acres of marsh and forest habitat, plus six
miles of easy-access boardwalk trails. More than 300 species have been observed here. "When
you're on the boardwalk, the birds will sometimes be only three or four feet away," Jim added. You
may not even need your binoculars. It almost overloads your senses, seeing all these tropical
migrants so close. You're like a kid in the candy store.

"There was one occasion when three buddies and I drove over to Magee, and it was pouring
down rain. Instead of hundreds of cars in the lot, there were only a few cars parked. We were right
on the shore of Lake Erie, with a buffer of trees before us where the trail begins. It was just getting to be light. There was a large fallen oak tree by the parking lot, mostly trunk and branches. It
must have had a lot of insects on it, as the oak was covered with warblers—twelve or thirteen different species, feeding actively, ignoring the rain. We were doing the same thing, sitting in the car
with our coffee. I guess the moral of this tale is, 'Don't let the weather deter you from going birding.'"

Birding, like other passionate pastimes, has the potential to bridge social and cultural
divides in the pursuit of mutual pleasure. Jim described one such phenomenon. "Back in the
mid-nineties, I began to notice that there were a number of Amish birders showing up in early
May along the shores of Lake Erie. The heart of Ohio Amish country is two hours (or more) from
the prime birding sites, so the Amish people would charter a van to take them north. (While
Amish do not generally drive internal-combustion vehicles, they are allowed to be passengers.)
The Amish birders come in their traditional garb—the women in bonnets and long dresses, the

OPPOSITE:
Chestnut-sided
Warblers are among
Lake Erie's many
spring visitors.

DESTINATION

37

men in straw hats and beards. Their children are along, too. They all have binoculars and bird guides along with everyone else. Some folks think that Amish people are against technology, but that's not true. They're against things that pull apart the family. Using binoculars is not anathema, as it helps them go birding—and birding is seen as something that brings their families together.

"These birding outings along Lake Erie are the only place I've ever seen outside of an Amish community where Amish folks are interacting with the general community. It's a perfect example of how birding can transcend cultural differences."

JIM BERRY is president of the Roger Tory Peterson Institute (www.rtpi.org), a national, non-profit nature education organization dedicated to continuing the legacy of Roger Tory Peterson by promoting the teaching and study of nature, and to thereby create knowledge of and appreciation and responsibility for the natural world.

IF YOU GO

➤ **Getting There:** The birding spots along Lake Erie are most easily reached from Cleveland, which is served by most major carriers.

➤ **Best Time to Visit:** Early May generally sees the peak of the spring migration. Lake Erie Wing Watch Weekend is held in mid-April of each year as a warm-up event.

➤ **Guides:** Lake Erie Wing Watch (www.lakeeriewingwatch.com) provides excellent background information for visiting birders.

➤ **Accommodations:** Lake Erie Wing Watch (www.lakeeriewingwatch.com) lists motels and hotels that offer discounts for visiting birders.

DESTINATION

37

MALHEUR NATIONAL WILDLIFE REFUGE

RECOMMENDED BY **Mike Houck**

Many picture Oregon as a wet place where towering Douglas firs draped in moss are perpetually enveloped in mist. While there are places west of the Cascade Mountains where this might be true at certain times of year, the Oregon east of the Cascades stands in sharp contrast. Here, rugged high desert badlands punctuated with isolated stands of tall mountains and the occasional rushing river are the norm—real Wild West scenery. One of the most remote and geographically staggering regions of eastern Oregon is that around Steens Mountain, and the Malheur National Wildlife Refuge. "I've led hundreds of birding tours in the region," Mike Houck began. "Some people certainly make the trip—a good six hours from Portland—to see specific birds. But most come to see birds against the backdrop of an extremely diverse, dramatic landscape."

The Malheur National Wildlife Refuge encompasses more than 187,000 acres of wetlands, meadows, riparian areas, and uplands in southeast Oregon, some thirty miles south of Burns, the only town of any size for a hundred miles. The most prominent landmark in the region—and the one most responsible for the region's diverse habitats—is Steens Mountain. This is the largest fault-block mountain in the Great Basin, formed when massive internal pressure forced the east edge upward along a fault line. It stretches thirty miles north to south, and rises to nearly 10,000 feet. The mountain acts as a great moisture collector, capturing the limited precipitation that moves east from the Pacific on its western slopes and channeling it to the creeks and streams that feed Malheur and Harney Lakes, two oases in these high desert environs. To the east of Steens Mountain rests the Alvord Desert, which sees a scant six inches of rain each year. While a variety of animals make Steens's "sky island" habitat their home (including bighorn sheep, pronghorn antelope, and Golden Eagles), most birding occurs in the marsh areas around the lakes and along the Donner und Blitzen River. (Visitors wandering south of the refuge along the Steens Loop Tour Route may encounter wild horses; a herd of nearly 300 mustangs makes this area their home.)

DESTINATION

38

Plans for the refuge were hatched by a prominent Portland resident named William Finley and the Portland Audubon Society at the turn of the last century. Plume hunters were decimating the populations of swans, herons, and other wading birds around Malheur Lake to meet the demand for feathers from milliners in the world's fashion centers. (At the time, an ounce of feathers commanded a higher price than an ounce of gold!) Finley was a close friend of then-President Theodore Roosevelt. "There's a story about when President Roosevelt came to Portland during a whistlestop tour," Mike continued. "All of Portland's politicos and business elite were there to greet the train, but Roosevelt is said to have ignored the entreaties of the dignitaries, instead calling out 'Get me Bill Finley!'" With Roosevelt's support, a bird reservation was created at Malheur Lake in 1908. During the depression, Civilian Conservation Corps workers constructed headquarters at the refuge, as well as the bridges, canals, and lookout towers that provide the main visitor infrastructure.

OPPOSITE:
The wetlands and Malheur Lake are fed by the Donner und Blitzen River, which flows off Steens Mountain.

Located along the Pacific Flyway and well endowed with both water and food, Malheur National Wildlife Refuge is a regular stop-off for a variety of migrants; 320 species have been recorded here. March sees a variety of waterfowl, ranging from Greater and Lesser Sandhill Cranes, Tundra Swans, and American White Pelicans to Long-billed Curlews and American Avocets. The northbound waterfowl migration is celebrated with the John Scharff Migratory Bird Festival each early April. As spring comes to the Steens/Malheur region, passerines arrive—warblers, tanagers, and buntings among them. Shorebirds beginning their journey south start arriving in mid-summer, followed by cranes, songbirds, and shorebirds. Good numbers of raptors also come through in the later fall, with Swainson's and Rough-legged Hawks among the group.

"I had two of my most memorable marsh-bird encounters at Malheur many years ago," Mike continued. "I was leading an Elderhostel trip to the region in the early 1980s. This was a time when the Malheur Basin had some very wet years, and Malheur and Harney Lakes flooded and were conjoined. The lakes so much resembled an inland sea during the early 1980s that we added Parasitic Jaegers and Ruddy Turnstones to our Malheur list. I was birding with our group of forty elders just east of the refuge headquarters, on a road that was nearly engulfed by the water. I heard the distinctive 'clicks' of a rail emanating from the marsh and shushed the group. At that moment, a beautiful Virginia Rail walked, chickenlike, up onto the road. The entire elder group froze, awestruck as the rail, in a herky-jerky strut, crossed the road not twenty feet from us.

"What happened next was truly remarkable. The rail, rather than simply crossing to reenter the marsh, made a ninety-degree turn and proceeded to walk our way. I asked everyone to freeze, be quiet, and watch. The rail proceeded to zig-zag between our legs, walking around our entire

DESTINATION

38

group before calmly descending back into the wetland.

"This should have been enough to make our day, but things got even more interesting. As we drove down the center patrol road, heading south into the heart of the refuge, I spotted something in the middle of the road, two or three hundred feet distant. I picked up my binoculars—steering the bus with one hand while trying to steady my binocs with the other—and sped up after realizing that we had an American Bittern walking right down the center of the road toward us. The entire elder group rushed to the front of the bus as we slowly crept toward the now-erect bittern. I told them to be sure to get a good look while the bittern still could be seen, as it would surely fly off into the marsh in a few moments. Amazingly, as we came within fifty feet of the bittern, it began flashing the bus with its white nuptial feathers that were now erect in one of the most spectacular mating—or was it territorial?—displays I've ever seen a bittern put on. It appeared the bittern saw our bus as one huge rival that it was not going to let pass. The bittern stood, neck stretched to the sky, white feathers flared on either side of its head, for a good five minutes. By then I'd shut the bus down and the entire group of elders, dead silent, watched in amazement. After I restarted the bus, the bittern apparently decided our coach was a bit much to take on, and lowering its neck, it walked Groucho Marx–style off the road and into the cattails."

MIKE HOUCK is executive director of the Urban Greenspaces Institute at the Portland State University Department of Geography, which he founded in 1999. He has been a leader at the local, regional, national, and international level in urban park and greenspace issues since 1980 when he founded the Urban Naturalist Program at the Audubon Society of Portland. Since that time, Mike has worked on urban parks, trails, greenspaces, and natural resources in the Portland-Vancouver metropolitan region. He speaks nationally and internationally on issues related to urban natural resources and sustainable development. He helped found the Coalition for a Livable Future (CLF) in 1994 to better integrate social and environmental issues into the region's growth management planning process. Mike was selected as a Loeb Fellow and spent a year in residence at Harvard's Graduate School of Design, focusing on urban planning and natural-resource protection. He continues in his role as Urban Naturalist at the Portland Audubon Society on a part-time basis. Mike serves on the national steering committee of the Ecological Cities Project of Amherst, MA. He also serves on several local and regional urban water quality and greenspace advisory committees in the Portland metropolitan region. An avid birder, Mike has visited Malheur (often leading Audubon trips) for thirty-seven years.

➤ **Getting There:** Malheur National Wildlife Refuge is approximately 325 miles southeast of Portland, which is served by most major carriers.

➤ **Best Time to Visit:** Spring songbird migration reaches its peak in mid-May; southbound shorebirds arrive in mid-summer; songbirds heading south reach a critical mass in September.

➤ **Guides:** Paradise Birding (541-549-8826; www.paradisebirding.com) leads spring and fall tours around Malheur. Wings Birding Tours (888-293-6443; wingsbirds.com) visits Malheur as part of an Oregon-wide tour.

➤ **Accommodations:** The Frenchglen Hotel (541-493-2825) is a popular stop for birders visiting Malheur and Steens Mountain. Harney County Chamber of Commerce (541-573-2636; www.harney county.com) lists other accommodations in the vicinity.

DESTINATION

38

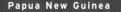
TARI VALLEY

RECOMMENDED BY **Jonathan Rossouw**

Birding paradise. Birds of Paradise. The two notions come together quite harmoniously in Papua New Guinea in the vicinity of Tari Valley. "Many consider Birds of Paradise the most exotic, fantastic birds on earth," Jonathan Rossouw began. "And there's no better place to see them than Papua New Guinea. I first visited the country after clients that I was guiding on a tour expressed interest in going. I'd heard a great deal about Ambua Lodge and Tari Valley over the years—after all, Phoebe Snetsinger, the woman who observed more birds than anyone else in the world, rated this place as her favorite spot on earth. There's simply no better place to see Birds of Paradise—as a group, they're so diverse in plumage, so diverse in their breeding displays. There's nothing that equals them in my mind, and this comes from someone who has spent most of his life birding in Africa and South America."

The nation of Papua New Guinea comprises the eastern half of New Guinea, a landmass northeast of Australia (the western half is called West Papua, and is a territory of Indonesia). Reference books often characterize New Guinea as the second-largest island in the world, although thanks to its size, cultural diversity, and biodiversity, many who know it well bristle at this factoid and think of New Guinea as a continent unto itself. Papua New Guinea—an area slightly larger than California—has over 850 indigenous languages, with most of its citizens living close to the land. (Contrary to tabloid perceptions, the majority of social groups here are not cannibalistic; the last recorded incident of cannibalism occurred in the early seventies, and even in earlier times, the cannibalism was limited to just a few tribes.) Papua New Guinea boasts one of the world's greatest levels of biodiversity. The varied landscape—ranging from lowland tropical rain forests to high montane cloud forests—is home to five to ten percent of the total species on the planet, many of which are endemic. According to the World Wildlife Fund, over 750 avian species have been observed on Papua New Guinea, with over 400 entirely restricted to the island.

OPPOSITE:
Spectacular Ribbon-tailed Astrapia can be encountered in the gardens of Ambua Lodge.

DESTINATION

39

Tari Valley is in the Southern Highlands region of Papua New Guinea, near the geographic center of the country. Above are the montane forests of Tari Gap at 7,000 feet, where Ambua Lodge is situated. In the valley are incredibly lush forests, a riot of greens punctuated by the bright hues of orchids and rhododendrons. "The excitement of Tari Valley begins when you land," Jonathan continued. "It's a private airstrip, and you land going uphill, which is an odd sensation. All around you there's montane forest. You eventually notice Ambua Lodge resting in a little clearing. There's immediately the sense that you've come to somewhere very special, and that sense is confirmed when you come upon the spectacular Ribbon-tailed Astrapia right in the gardens of the lodge."

Ribbon-tailed Astrapia is one of forty-two species of Birds of Paradise, a fantastical group of birds found on New Guinea and in Northeastern Australia; thirty-six Birds of Paradise are endemic to New Guinea. Related to crows, different species of "BOP" (as they are affectionately known) range sea level to elevations of almost 10,000 feet. Some BOPs feed primarily on fruit, others primarily on arthropods. For a number of species, little definitive information about feeding habits (or anything else) is available. One thing is certainly true: nearly all the males of the species are famous for their splendid plumage. For thousands of years, their plumes have been interwoven with the lives of native New Guineans, who incorporate the feathers and skins of BOPs into elaborate headdresses. "In the Tari Valley, you can visit a tribal group called the Huli Wigmen," Jonathan continued. "They create the most ornate headdresses you can imagine, using feathers from Astrappins, Raggianna, and Blue Birds of Paradise, amongst others. The annual gatherings of the tribes, known locally as Sing-Songs, where thousands of warriors meet to show off their finery, are one of the world's great cultural and ornithological displays."

Once the feathers of BOPs were discovered by the outside world, a thriving trade in the plumes evolved. Records show that BOP feathers were prized in Asia some 2000 years ago. Word of their wonders did not reach the Western world until 1520, when the Sultan of Batchian (an island in the Malay Archipelago) presented explorer Ferdinand Magellan with several skins to pass along to his benefactor, the king of Spain. The skins had the birds' feet and wings removed. When sailors asked residents on adjoining islands how the birds lived, they were told that the birds floated in the skies and subsisted on dew. It took over a century for this tale to be debunked. Not long after BOPs were identified as creatures of the earth, demand for their feathers in the West escalated. Somewhat astonishingly, legal trade in skins and feathers was banned in Europe and the United States in the early twentieth century, before these incredible creatures could be pushed to the brink of extinction. Most of the species populations are healthy today due in large part to the fact that only adult males are hunted for plumes.

"Around Tari Valley, you can see thirteen species of BOP, both species that you'd find in the higher altitudes like King of Saxony Birds of Paradise and Brown Sicklebill and lower-altitude species," Jonathan continued. "You can go down to the valley where the Huli people have their fields and find the display grounds of Blue Birds of Paradise, Stephanie's Astrapia, and Lawes's Parutia. Many people consider the Resplendent Quetzal to be the most beautiful bird in the New World. For me, the iridescence of Stephanie's Astrapia—a jet-black bird with a brilliant green head and long tail shot with purple—is every bit as spectacular.

"I'll never forget the sight of a King of Saxony Bird of Paradise on its display perch near Tari Gap. This bird has incredibly long plumes that come from the back of its head. When it's displaying, the male bobs back and forth, then suddenly leans forward, dropping its plumes over its head, and moving them vigorously from side to side. It's an almost unbelievable sight; if it doesn't move you to become a passionate birder, nothing will.

"It can be difficult to get past the attraction of Birds of Paradise, but the wonders go on and on. You have flocks of colorful Lorikeets, and strange Tiger-Parrots, oddities like Tit Berrypecker and the bizarre Wattled Ploughbill, and skulkers like Spotted Jewel-Babbler and Blue-Breasted Pitta. If you're lucky, you might come upon New Guinea Harpy-Eagle or even Shovel-billed Kingfisher. One great curiosity is the Blue-capped Ifrita. This bird has toxic plumage, similar to that secreted by the Colombian poison dart frog. It's believed that they sequester the toxins from the beetles they eat. The excellent local guides at Ambua know where to search for these birds; if you visit Ambua, you're likely to find a number of these exotic creatures with their help."

JONATHAN ROSSOUW is a native South African and a trip leader and partner with the Seattle-based travel company, Zegrahm Expeditions (www.zeco.com). He is busy throughout the year either scouting new destinations for or leading travelers through remote locales around the globe, pointing out and lecturing about the wildlife along the way. In 2005, Jonathan recorded sightings of a record-breaking 3,024 birds; he has observed over 7,000 birds in his more than twenty-five years in the field. A medical doctor by training, Jonathan has had a lifelong interest in wildlife, which has resulted in extensive periods living, working, and traveling throughout Africa, Asia, and the Americas. Currently he spends the majority of his time engaged in wildlife projects, which include leading tours to such diverse areas as Madagascar and India and conducting ornithological surveys in Uganda and Mozambique. Jonathan is equally enthusiastic about mammals as about his specialties, birds and reptiles; indeed, he has an infectious curiosity and passion for all aspects of natural history. He has coauthored birding guides to Uganda and Southern Africa.

DESTINATION 39

175

➤ **Getting There:** First, you'll need to reach Mt. Hagen, which is served by Air Niugini from Port Moresby, PNG; Port Moresby can be reached via Brisbane on Air Niguini; Brisbane is served by several carriers, including American and Qantas. From Mt. Hagen, you'll need to take a charter flight to Ambua Lodge (the lodge can make arrangements).

➤ **Best Time to Visit:** The highlands region around Ambua has pleasant temperatures between 50 and 80 degrees; there's often a shower in the late afternoon. Weather is constant most of the year, as is the bird life.

➤ **Guides:** Ambua Lodge (see below) has guides available. Several tour companies lead general trips to Papua New Guinea that include stops in the Tari Valley, including Field Guides (800-728-4953; www.fieldguides.com), Victor Emanuel Nature Tours (800-328-8368; www.ventbirds.com), and Wings Birding Tours (888-293-6443; wingsbirds.com).

➤ **Accommodations:** Ambua Lodge (+675 542-1438; www.pngtours.com) is the venue for birders visiting Tari Valley and Tari Gap.

HAWK MOUNTAIN SANCTUARY

RECOMMENDED BY **Scott Weidensaul**

"I was the sort of kid that was always dragging snakes and salamanders home," Scott Weidensaul recalled. "I was interested in nature of all sorts. I grew up not far from Hawk Mountain, but had never been there, though I'd been bugging my parents to take me. One fall day when I was about twelve, we were off from school, and it looked as though my little sister and I would kill each other. My mom decided to take us to Hawk Mountain so we wouldn't do so. It happened to be a perfect migration day, with the passage of a cold front and accompanying northwest winds. We hiked up the trail to the top of Kittatinny Ridge. You come out above a boulder field, an 800- or 1000-foot drop. On the ridge, the birds come right at you; they're at eye level or below. Everywhere you look, there are hawks. I had my *Golden Guide to Birds* and some cheapo binoculars. None of the real birds looked like the birds in my book, but I was calling out the names, nonetheless. There was an older woman sitting next to me, listening to me as I was calling them out, and finally, she turned around and said, 'Son, sit down, you don't know what you're talking about.' And then she started to teach me how accipiters flap and then sail, and how a Red-shouldered Hawk's wings droop when it glides. These were my first halting steps toward learning hawk identification.

"Once I got my driver's license, I would go up to Hawk Mountain constantly. One of the things about the raptor migration that fired my young imagination was the notion that the world was funneling through my backyard. Broad-winged Hawks from Quebec going to Guatemala, Merlins from Labrador heading to Mexico. It was mind-bending stuff for a kid."

Hawk Mountain Sanctuary rests on Kittatinny Ridge, a 185-mile-long mountain chain along the southeastern spine of the Appalachian Mountains in southeastern Pennsylvania, just west of Allentown. The sanctuary itself is 2,600 acres, but it's adjoined by another 13,000 acres of protected land, comprising the largest contiguous forest in the region. In the fall, from the northwest when the winds are blowing, they hit the ridge and create updrafts that allow the raptors to sail easily

DESTINATION

40

along the ridge, right past North Lookout, the main viewing area. "To see the big show at Hawk Mountain, it's extremely important that you have wind," Scott continued. "On a day without wind, there will be little but turkey vultures there." For Scott, one of the most engaging facets of Hawk Mountain is the ever-changing face of the migration. "First you have Bald Eagles and ospreys in late August; by the middle of September, there's a flood of Broad-winged Hawks. Their numbers drop off as Cooper's Hawks and Sharp-shinned Hawks build in early October; as they drop, numbers of Goshawks and Red-tailed Hawks and Golden Eagles build in November. In the beginning of the season, you're drenched in sweat, trying to keep the yellowjackets at bay. By end of season, you're carrying up a sleeping bag, trying to keep yourself warm."

The story of how Hawk Mountain Sanctuary came to be is in part the tale of Rosalie Edge—a woman who used her connections and wealth to will the sanctuary into being. (She was also instrumental in helping establish Olympic, King's Canyon, and Sequoia National Parks.) "Rosalie Edge was a New York socialite who'd been a leader in the suffrage movement," Scott continued. "You get insight into her character by the fact that the president of the National Audubon Society called her a scold, and she took this as a compliment. Around 1930, word was going around in birding circles about this mountaintop in Pennsylvania where hunters would go to shoot hawks. A conservationist named Dick Pough collected hundreds of dead hawks and photographed them, hoping to interest someone in doing something. He went to the National Audubon Society, but they dragged their feet. The photographs eventually made their way to Rosalie Edge, and she sprang into action. She created what she called the Emergency Conservation Committee and in 1934 bought the mountain, creating the world's first refuge for birds of prey—which were viewed as enemies by many in the general population, and by many ornithologists as well. She hired a fellow from Cape Cod named Maurice Broun to oversee the sanctuary. Maurice had a petite wife named Irma. While Maurice was up on the lookout counting hawks, little Irma held the gunners at bay. Many were big, stocky coalminers or farmers of Pennsylvania Dutch stock, and none too happy to have their hunting spot taken away. But Irma would tell them they couldn't go up on the mountain with their guns.

"I grew up—most of us did—with the image of birders being slightly dweeby, nerdy people, like Ms. Jane Hathaway on The Beverly Hillbillies," Scott continued. "On Hawk Mountain, I met birders who faced down armed men. These people weren't milquetoasts. I saw early on what it means to put oneself on the line for conservation. The ripples from Hawk Mountain have spread everywhere; it's the mother church of raptor conservation and research, and the model established here has been copied around the world."

OPPOSITE:
The view from North Lookout on Hawk Mountain.

DESTINATION

40

There can be two or three thousand people on Hawk Mountain on a warm day in September. But when the mercury dips, the numbers thin out—and that's okay by Scott. "It's kind of nice to have just a handful of rugged diehards up there," Scott said. And he shared a favorite cold-weather memory of Hawk Mountain. "It was a Thanksgiving Day about fifteen years ago, and there were snow squalls up on the mountain. There were just one or two other people up there. The snow would roll in for five or six minutes, and there would be a whiteout. The snow was moving to the east, the same direction from where the hawks were coming, though there weren't too many coming through, just a few Red-taileds and Northern Harriers. As one of the squalls went through, a huge Golden Eagle materialized out of the snow. It was right there before me, elemental, as though conjured up from the wind and snow. I have such vivid memories of that bird. I can recall every detail."

SCOTT WEIDENSAUL is an author and naturalist who has written more than two dozen books on natural history, including *Living on the Wind: Across the Hemisphere with Migratory Birds*, a Pulitzer Prize finalist; *The Ghost with Trembling Wings*, about the search for species that may or may not be extinct; and his most recent book, *Return to Wild America: A Yearlong Search for the Continent's Natural Soul*. He lectures widely on wildlife and environmental topics, and is an active field researcher, specializing in birds of prey and hummingbirds. He lives in the Appalachians of eastern Pennsylvania, not far from Hawk Mountain.

IF YOU GO

▶ **Getting There:** Hawk Mountain Sanctuary is seven miles north of Hamburg, Pennsylvania, roughly two hours northwest of Philadelphia (served by most major carriers), and one hour northeast of Harrisburg (served by many carriers, including American Eagle, Continental, and Delta).

▶ **Best Time to Visit:** Hawk migration is under way from mid-August to early December, and mid to late October tends to see the greatest raptor variety.

▶ **Guides:** At the height of the migration, many volunteer hawk counters are working on Hawk Mountain, and will be happy to share their raptor knowledge.

▶ **Accommodations:** The Hawk Mountain Sanctuary website (www.hawkmountain.org) lists nearby lodgings options.

TARIFA

RECOMMENDED BY **David Allen Sibley**

"I love bird migration," David Sibley began. "I think it's the aspect of birding that excites me most. My favorite spots are those where you can see migrations from one place and watch them stream by. When I first went to Europe back in the late eighties, I was very curious to see southern Spain. Partially it was for the notoriety of Gibraltar. But I also knew vaguely that the very tip of Spain— a place called Tarifa—was a great funnel for migrating birds crossing to and fro from Europe and Africa."

Tarifa rests at the southern tip of the Cádiz province overlooking the Straits of Gibraltar, a narrow stretch of the Mediterranean Sea separating Europe from Morocco and the African continent. At the straits' narrowest point, the continents are only six miles apart. This is the single most significant migratory path for Central and Western European migrants, and as such draws visitors (avian and human) in the spring and fall. Spain's Costa del Sol—to the east in the Málaga province—has attracted a great deal of tourist development in recent years, at times summoning comparisons to the French Riviera. The sea front from Tarifa northwest to the city of Cádiz— which has been dubbed Costa de la Luz—has thus far escaped overdevelopment, though how long that will last is uncertain. "It was quite reminiscent of the coast of southern California before it became so crowded," David continued. "It's rural, chaparral country, with mountains climbing right up from the coastline. There's also lagoon habitat, and pine forests. Standing on the beach, you look up at rocky hills that extend up 500 feet. When I was there one October, there were Griffon Vultures and other raptors circling in the hills, and flock after flock of diurnal songbirds coming down the beach in a continuous stream. You can often see the northern hills of Morocco from Tarifa. Watching bird migration is such a powerful connection to the cycles of seasons and to all the places that the birds travel. And Tarifa is a very dramatic place to imagine these birds, like their ancestors for thousands of years, crossing from one continent to another."

DESTINATION

41

Coto Doñana National Park, just to the north and west of Tarifa, is a significant stopover point for migrants, and boasts a healthy number of resident species, including a colony of some fifteen pairs of Spanish Imperial Eagles, which are numbered at less than 500 in the world. The park, which encompasses 500 square miles of *marismas* (coastal marshes that dry up in the summer), Mediterranean scrublands, and dunes, is considered one of Western Europe's last great wilderness regions; the World Wildlife Fund estimates that over six million birds light here during their migration. Regional specialties that might be encountered here include Red-crested Pochard, Marbled Duck, Red-knobbed Coot, Purple Swamphen, and Yellow Wagtail. The wetlands at Coto Doñana attract Greater Flamingos, Spoonbills, and Glossy Ibis, among other waders. White and Black Storks are frequently encountered as well.

The territory of Gibraltar, just east of Tarifa, is another popular birding spot, especially for British citizens who tend to show up in the spring. "Gibraltar is a small detour off the main migration route," David continued. "While some migrants pass by Gibraltar, it's not like Tarifa in terms of seeing streams of birds passing by. Birding possibilities aside, I have to say that Gibraltar is a bizarre little place. We pulled in there and went through customs, and all of a sudden, it was as if we were in England. There were fish and chips joints, British newspapers, bobbies patrolling around. Relative to Tarifa and Andalucia, it's very crowded and very developed." [Gibraltar is in fact an overseas territory of the United Kingdom, and as such has been a point of contention since Spain ceded sovereignty in 1713. The rock of the same name—also called the Pillars of Hercules—climbs to nearly 1,400 feet, and doubtless provides a navigational reference point for migrants.]

Some birding locales are enchanting because birders can have a reasonable expectation of what they will encounter there. Part of the appeal of migration hotspots—be they High Island, Cape May, or Tarifa—is the thrill of never knowing exactly what will show up. "I recall sitting at the edge of some dunes at an estuary at Tarifa," David said. "There were a variety of finches streaming by, as well as wagtails, swallows, and other species. When I turned my binoculars to the hills behind me, there were kettles of raptors circling upward. When they got enough altitude, they'd head out across the straits. In the middle of all of this activity, a spoonbill came flying by. It flew down over the beach, circled a few times, then landed in the estuary; it ended up staying for several days. It was one of those experiences I love about migration hotspots. You just sit and wait and watch the spectacle, never knowing exactly what will show up."

DAVID ALLEN SIBLEY, son of the well-known ornithologist Fred Sibley, began seriously watching and drawing birds in 1969, at age seven. He has gone on to become one of America's most celebrated birding artists and writers. Since 1980 David has traveled the continent watching birds on his own and as a tour leader for WINGS, Inc. His best-selling books include *The Sibley Guide to Birds*, *The Sibley Field Guide to Birds of Eastern North America*, *The Sibley Field Guide to Birds of Western North America*, *The Sibley Guide to Bird Life & Behavior*, *Sibley's Birding Basics*, *Birds of Cape May*, and *Hawks in Flight*. He lives in Concord, Massachusetts.

IF YOU GO

► **Getting There:** Most travelers will fly into Sevilla (which is served by many carriers, including American, Continental, and United) and then drive the 120 miles south to Tarifa.
► **Best Time to Visit:** Spring and fall migration: March through April and September through November.
► **Guides:** Doñana Bird Tours (+34 955-755-460; www.donanabirdtours.com) is a local birding tour guide. Bird Holidays (+44 113-3910-510; www.birdholidays.co.uk) from England leads week-long tours to the region.
► **Accommodations:** Accommodations around Tarifa are highlighted at http://tarifa.costasur.com/en. A popular birders' retreat near Coto Doñana National Park is Hotel Toruño (+33 959-44-2323); some rooms look out over the *marismas*.

SERENGETI NATIONAL PARK

RECOMMENDED BY **Carter Roberts**

The Great Migration, where nearly two million ungulates mass for a five-hundred-mile journey. Large prides of lions, lazing in the midday sun or picking at a kill. A herd of elephants moving slowly by, so close you can smell them. Heady spectacles indeed. But not all the action in the Serengeti is on the ground.

"If you can tear your eyes away from the lions and zebras and giraffes, the Serengeti has the most beautiful assemblage of birds," Carter Roberts began. "Lilac-crested Rollers, a variety of hornbills, lovebirds, hulking Martial Eagles, just for starters. Visitors expect to see great mammals—they don't expect the glittering array of birds. I have to say that it's some of the easiest and most spectacular birding in the world."

Vast seems like an understatement when referencing Tanzania's Serengeti National Park, the seemingly endless savanna that unfolds north to south in the Great Rift Valley, east of Lake Victoria and south of the border with Kenya. (Serengeti is the Maasai term for "flat endless plains.") The park itself—5,675 square miles—is bigger than the state of Connecticut. When this land is combined with adjacent park and reserve holdings—Arush, Maasai Mara, Tarangire, Lake Manyara, and Ngorongoro—it begins to take on the size of much of New England! The Serengeti includes woodland habitat and riparian areas, but it's the savanna that grips the imagination. "The savanna of the Serengeti is one of the world's classic, iconic landscapes," Carter continued. "When you see the long grasses and unique acacia trees, you have an almost unconscious association with the place. Every part of the landscape has its own array of birds, and this always surprises people."

Carter paused for a moment, and then added, "Africa is a continent that profoundly moves men's souls. It has extreme poverty, but also incredible beauty. The World Wildlife Fund has identified eastern Africa as one of the world's great conservation opportunities. You have astonishing concentrations of different mammals, birds, and plants, and it's also a place where models are

OPPOSITE:
The Secretarybird, a resident of Serengeti National Park that you're almost sure to see.

DESTINATION

42

185

being developed that balance the needs of people and their livelihoods with big, intact tracts of land. Everyone—from ordinary tourists to political leaders from around the world—come away inspired and dedicated to helping address Africa's greater issues."

Most birders who visit the Serengeti do so in the company of an organized tour, and tour operators will allow several days to explore each of the park's special regions—the western corridor and Grumetti River, the Seronera River Valley, and Ndutu, to mention a few. It's not uncommon for visitors to come away with 400 (or more) species from the park, including three of Tanzania's endemics, the Fischer's Lovebird, Rufous-tailed Weaver, and Gray-breasted Spurfowl, plus specialties like the Silverbird and Usambiro Barbet. Whatever your itinerary, operators will detour your 4-WD caravan to take in the Great Migration, truly one of the wonders of the natural world. Even the most rabid birder will not be disappointed by the mammalian diversion, though in truth, by taking in the spectacle of the migration, one will also see many new birds.

It begins when more than one million wildebeest start massing in the southeastern section of the park in February or March to give birth to their calves. The wildebeest are joined by a half-million Thomson's gazelle and a quarter-million zebra—and thousands of predators, from prides of lions and packs of hyenas and jackals to cheetahs and leopards—all drawn together to act out an age-old ecosystem drama. Once the calves are old enough to walk, the assorted herbivores will begin their slow trek west and north, following the life-giving rains that rejuvenate the grasslands. The grand entourage of grazers and carnivores makes their way north to the Mara area in Kenya, with the big cats picking off young or weaker animals, leaving morsels for vultures, jackals, and other scavengers. After a short hiatus, the troupe moves slowly back toward Ndutu, where the whole process will begin again.

Several avian species of the Serengeti stand out for Carter. "The Ground Hornbills and vast flocks of flamingoes on some of the lakes were moving sights for me," Carter said. "I was also taken with the Secretarybird. I would describe it as a raptor on stilts. It has amazing plumage, with these quills fanned out behind its neck. I was startled at how quickly it could run." Secretarybirds are tall, with a body length reaching five feet; they have the longest legs of any member of the raptor family, which enable them to achieve such impressive land speed. (Their long legs also come in handy when hunting; Secretarybirds often neutralize the small mammals, reptiles, and amphibians they prey on with a quick kick.) The moniker "Secretarybird" is believed to have come from the resemblance the bird's head feathers bear to the quill pens a Dickensian-era clerk might have stored behind his ear.

"On my last trip to the Serengeti, my group was treated to a balloon ride," Carter continued. "You take off at daybreak. The balloons rise to about forty feet in the air, and then the operators let the breeze take you sailing across the grasslands. We saw a great deal of mammal and bird life from our floating perch, including Splendid Starlings and Martial Eagles. But the Secretarybirds had me in awe. A pair we came upon seemed to be chasing us. When we touched down, our hosts had a nice bottle of Champagne waiting for us. We filled our glasses and toasted the Secretarybird!"

CARTER ROBERTS is president and CEO of the World Wildlife Fund (www.worldwildlife.org). He joined the World Wildlife Fund in February 2004 as chief conservation officer and COO. Prior to joining WWF, Carter was vice president for Strategic Planning and Global Priorities at the Nature Conservancy. As vice president for The Nature Conservancy's Central America Division, he opened new offices across the region and oversaw operations in six countries. From 1990 to 1996, he was TNC's state director for Massachusetts. Earlier in his career, Carter led marketing and management teams at Procter & Gamble and Gillette. He holds an M.B.A. from Harvard Business School and graduated with honors from Princeton University. Fluent in Spanish and an avid birder, Carter is married and has three young children.

IF YOU GO

▶ **Getting There:** Visitors to the Serengeti generally fly in to Kilamanjaro International Airport near Arusha, Tanzania, which is served by Kenya Airways via Amsterdam.
▶ **Best Time to Visit:** While birding is consistent throughout the year, most wish to visit during the periods of the Great Migration—May through October, and December.
▶ **Guides:** Many companies offer general safaris in the Serengeti. Fewer offer bird-focused tours, though such expeditions are offered by Victor Emanuel Nature Tours (800-328-8368; www.ventbirds.com).
▶ **Accommodations:** The Serengeti National Park website (www.serengeti.org) lists the many lodges in the park; it also advises visitors to book with tour operators who can take care of all the logistical details, including lodgings.

DESTINATION

42

HIGH ISLAND TO GALVESTON

RECOMMENDED BY **Kevin T. Karlson**

New visitors to High Island may be surprised to find that it is not an island at all, but rather an elevated salt dome on the Bolivar Peninsula, east of Houston. At thirty-eight feet above sea level, it's the highest land mass between the Yucatán Peninsula and Mobile, Alabama. If conditions are right in the spring, it can be one of the most exciting birding spots in the world.

"I believe that the Upper Texas Coast, from High Island to Galveston, is the finest migratory location in North America," Kevin Karlson declared. "No other place combines the movement of songbirds with such a fantastic collection of herons, egrets, gulls, and terns. The trees on High Island act like magnets for the birds coming from the Yucatán, making the spot stand out from the thousands of miles of adjacent coastal marsh. If you get storm conditions, you can expect large fallouts of migratory birds. The fallouts are not what they used to be. Those that didn't experience the neotropic songbirds migration thirty years ago have no comparison to what's going on today in terms of regularity and numbers. Then again, the older guys told me that when I came along twenty-eight years ago. In my mind, it's still impressive."

In late winter/early spring, neotropical migrant birds that have been wintering in Central and South America begin their push north toward nesting grounds. Eventually, many birds reach an important migratory "jump-off point" in the vicinity of the Yucatán Peninsula. Their next push brings them up to 600 miles across the Gulf of Mexico; with good conditions, the trip takes roughly eighteen hours, which brings them to Texas from late morning to mid-afternoon. While some birds may briefly linger on the coast after their passage, others will continue migrating after nightfall—unless they encounter stormy north winds. These winds can lead to the "fallouts" that Kevin described. Exhausted by their struggle against the elements, the migrants seek respite at the first available shelter . . . which more often than not is High Island. You never know what might blow in during a High Island fallout, but based on counts from 2006, you're likely to come upon

OPPOSITE:
Resident Great Blue Herons are joined by songbirds during High Island's infamous spring fallouts.

D E S T I N A T I O N

43

a plethora of warblers, tanagers, grosbeaks, kingbirds, orioles, cuckoos, catbirds, vireos, and buntings—for starters.

"The beautiful part about spring around the Upper Texas Coast is that even if you don't get a migratory wind, there are still numerous nesting birds," Kevin continued. "At a place like Cape May, if you don't get a fallout, there's not much to look at until the nesting birds set up territory. Along the Upper Texas coast, you'll get nesting songbirds, herons, terns, etc. You're just not going to have a bad day."

Birders visiting this part of the world in the spring have one serious impasse to overcome: where to focus their efforts. From Anahuac National Wildlife Refuge in the north to Galveston Island in the south, there's over forty miles of excellent and varied habitat. As tempting as it might be to hunker down on High Island to see what might blow in, you'd be selling yourself short to do so. Kevin offered an itinerary that might take the better part of April and May to complete.

"Just north of High Island there's Anahuac National Wildlife Refuge, where there's managed freshwater habitat as well as a saltwater area. Shorebirds often frequent the freshwater habitat, as do other birds such as American Bitterns, Least Bitterns, and King Rails. You'll also get some impressive songbird fallouts in the spring in various fragmented woodland habitats. There are raptors here, too. If you move a bit inland from the coast, you'll find many rice fields. These are important locations for Golden Plovers, Buff-breasted Sandpipers, and other grassland shore-birds. Some of the rice fields are managed to make sure there's habitat for migratory shorebirds.

"As you drive down the coast, you'll also get grassland shorebirds, including Upland Sandpipers, in short-grass pastureland along the side of the road. Barn Owls might be hunting in the afternoon, and there's a chance you'll encounter songbirds too. Just this side of Galveston you'll come to what I believe is the finest shorebird sanctuary in all of North America—Bolivar Flats and Horseshoe Marsh." The Bolivar Flats/Horseshoe Marsh complex is a huge expanse of mud flats that was created by jetties that were constructed a hundred years ago to protect the entrance to Galveston Bay. The area is of such great importance to shorebirds that it has been des-ignated a site of hemispheric importance by the Western Hemisphere Shorebird Reserve Network. "There are incredible concentrations of shorebirds all year—late spring, fall, even winter—but particularly in spring. If it weren't for the Houston Audubon Society, I imagine that the Bolivar area would be overrun with development and subject to daily disturbance.

"Bolivar Flats has provided so many magical migration moments during my many visits, with amazing concentrations of bird numbers and species. One day it might be twenty-six Yellow Crown Night Herons landing on the beach to rest, or the 10,000 Avocets that came and decided

DESTINATION

43

to feed right in front of me in a synchronous fashion, while 150 White Pelicans sat in the distance on the horizon. It's surreal to see such concentrations, while on my right, harriers are cruising, Long-bill Curlews are flying by, and Whimbrels are calling. I've had 2,500 Black Terns resting on the beach, while I photographed shorebirds on adjacent mudflats forty feet away. You'll get a great variety of terns there as well—Sandwich, Least, Forster's, Common, Caspian, Royal, Black, Gull-billed, and Black Skimmer—you can compare them side by side. It's almost too good to be true. You leave there, your head is spinning on a late April or May day, or an early fall day."

The fun doesn't stop when you reach Galveston. "There's East Beach, on the northeast section of Galveston Island," Kevin continued. "You'll get good concentrations of shorebirds in winter and during migrations. Each spring, Long-billed and Short-billed Dowitchers may be seen side by side. Behind East Beach's Big Reef Nature Park, there exists a combination of grassland and marsh habitat, which provides nesting grounds for a variety of shorebirds, herons, egrets, raptors, and songbirds. At the sign for Big Reef Nature Park, walk over a little bridge and you can access the water where the Gulf of Mexico meets Galveston Bay. It's the busiest shipping channel in North America, but there's still a fantastic assortment of coastal wildlife—White Pelicans in the winter, Brown Pelicans, Red-breasted Mergansers; a Kelp Gull was there a few years ago. During migration, you'll get a mix of everything. I'll stand there for an hour, and twenty Black Terns will come past, then maybe ten Golden Plovers and many other migrant birds."

Galveston toasts its avian abundance each spring with FeatherFest, a celebration of the birds of the Upper Texas coastal area. Should you attend, you're almost sure to find Kevin there, leading tours.

KEVIN T. KARLSON has been a wildlife photographer for twenty-six years and active as a birder for twenty-nine. He has traveled from the wilds of the Alaskan Arctic to the rain forests of Central and South America to photograph birds. Kevin's work has been widely published in birding magazines and journals, as well as books, field guides, calendars, and CD-ROMs. In 1999, Tidemark Press published Kevin's own calendar titled "Birds of the Arctic Tundra," which was endorsed by the American Birding Association. He worked closely with Peter Thayer in a major revision of the CD-ROM *The Cornell Lab of Ornithology's Guide to Birds of North America* as head ornithologist, photo researcher, and submitter of almost 800 photos used in the project. Kevin is currently on the advisory board of *Wild Bird* magazine as well as a staff contributor of the column "Birder's ID." Kevin has authored numerous articles on birds, and recently completed *The Shorebird Guide* (Houghton Mifflin Co., 2006, with coauthors Richard Crossley and Michael O'Brien), a compre-

DESTINATION

43

hensive field guide with 700 photos that outline a simpler method of bird identification for beginners and experts alike. He is a frequent keynote speaker on the Birding Symposium and Festival Circuit. Kevin is the founder and president of Jaeger Tours, Inc., a small birding-tour company (www.jaegertours.net) with an emphasis on the enjoyment of a total birding/nature experience.

IF YOU GO

➤ **Getting There:** Birders traversing the coastline from High Island to Galveston will usually fly into Houston.

➤ **Best Time to Visit:** Mid-April to early May is traditionally the peak time for spring migration. An annual celebration of the region's avian abundance, FeatherFest, is held in Galveston in late March/early April.

➤ **Guides:** Most of the major birding-tour companies lead trips to the Upper Texas Coast during spring migration. Do-it-yourselfers will find an abundance of good information to point them in the right direction, including the notes at Texas Birding (www.texasbirding.net) and at the Great Texas Coastal Birding Trails website (www.tpwd.state.tx.us), sponsored by the Texas Parks & Wildlife Department.

➤ **Accommodations:** Several venues favored by birding-tour companies are the Holiday Inn Express in Winnie (409-296-2866) and the Los Patos Lodge in Humble (281-852-6456) around High Island. For accommodations in Galveston, consult the Galveston Island Convention and Visitors Bureau (888-939-8680; www.galveston.com).

DESTINATION

43

LOWER RIO GRANDE VALLEY

RECOMMENDED BY **Paul J. Baicich**

While most would agree that the world has become smaller and international travel has become easier, there are still many people who feel most comfortable on their home turf. For the birder interested in seeing varietals of Mexican lineage without actually venturing south of the border, there is the Lower Rio Grande Valley in southeastern Texas. "It's not necessarily better than places in nearby Mexico (like the Monterey area)," said Paul Baicich, "but it's the northernmost area where birds of so-called Mexican character come in. And it's in the USA."

The Lower Rio Grande Valley is geographically blessed from a birding perspective, as both the Central and Mississippi flyways funnel through the region. Combine this with a convergence of climates—desert, temperate, subtropic, and coastal—and one can understand why nearly 500 species can be found in the valley, not to mention the chance for megararities. The Lower Rio Grande Valley National Wildlife Refuge is a growing patchwork of riparian forest, dry chaparral bush, freshwater marshes, and coastal wetlands. It stretches some 275 river miles, from the Falcon Dam just beyond Roma, Texas, to Brownsville, where the Rio Grande enters the Gulf of Mexico. The refuge, which connects many modest-size patches of land along the river's north shore en route to the sea, is as much a testament to the possibilities of public/private partnerships (spear-headed by the U.S. Fish and Wildlife Service) as it is to ecological farsightedness.

"My first visit to the Lower Rio Grande Valley was a mind-blowing experience," Paul continued. "It was 1966, and a good friend of mine was going to attend graduate school in Austin. He invited me to go along for the ride from New York, saying we could bird around Texas before his classes began. We birded at a number of spots, including Big Bend National Park, but the Lower Rio Grande was the highlight. At that time, the corridor wasn't very tourist-friendly. It was really a ranching/farming backwater, and there were hardly any motels. That's changed significantly. The communities along the river have accommodated themselves for ecotravelers, especially

from November to April. From Mission to McAllen to Harlingen, they're ready for both snow-birds and snowbirders. When a truly rare bird shows up, it can be a windfall as the birders follow. It's hard to dismiss the possibility that chambers of commerce have brought the birds in!"

There are a number of parks and preserves along the Lower Rio Grande Valley. The Bentsen-Rio Grande Valley State Park is one hotspot. Here, the floodplain forests that once characterized much of the river corridor are still largely intact, attracting many of the specialty birds the region is known for. (Channelizing of the Rio Grande and other flood control measures have devastated much of the riparian forest that historically graced its banks; attempts are being made to period-ically flood surrounding lands at some sites in an effort to revive these forests.) Some regular res-idents of interest to traveling birders include Plain Chachalacas, Altamira Orioles, Northern Beardless Tyrannulet, and Green Jays. Bentsen is also the headquarters of the World Birding Center, a network of nine sites along the length of the lower valley, from Roma to South Padre Island by the Gulf. The World Birding Center, along with the Great Texas Birding Trail (which highlights a variety of do-it-yourself birding routes in the state's most bird-rich areas) have done a great deal to promote the south Texas region as a major birding destination. The Texas Parks and Wildlife Department will also cooperate with a number of birding festivals in the valley throughout the year, providing a focal point for visitors and local birders alike.

One of Paul's favorite spots is the Santa Ana National Wildlife Refuge, south of McAllen. "Santa Ana is clearly one of the gems of the refuge system," Paul said. "It has the thorn forest habi-tat that's gone from so much of the region. Walking along trails that fringe ponds on the refuge, there are ebony trees on one side, hanging with Spanish moss; on the other side, there are cac-tuses. It's a lovely, exotic place with many semitropical qualities. There's always interesting bird life there, including Great Kiskadee, Couch's Kingbird, Brown-crested Flycatcher, Olive Sparrow, and White-tipped Dove—and sometimes, Hook-billed Kite. At Santa Ana, you get a real feeling for what the valley must have been like decades ago." The refuge is also home to nearly half of all butterfly species found in the United States.

As mentioned above, the Lower Rio Grande Valley has a great reputation for drawing rari-ties, birds that are unlikely to show up anywhere else in the United States. Those rarities draw the faithful. "I love visiting the valley any time. But whenever I venture down to see a specialty bird — be it a White-throated Robin, Crimson-collared Grosbeak, Blue Bunting, or Golden-crowned Warbler—I bump into acquaintances whom I haven't seen for several years, friends from Michigan, California, Ohio. They've come for the same reason that I'm there, and it's always a sociable—though impromptu—get-together. Roger Tory Peterson used to call it the Field Glass

OPPOSITE:

Altamira Orioles are a Lower Rio Grande Valley resident of interest to visitors.

DESTINATION

44

195

Fraternity. Running into these friends at a place like the Lower Rio Grande is a pleasant expression of the camaraderie and fellowship that develops among active birders over the years."

PAUL J. BAICICH has been an active birder since his early teens in New York City. At the American Birding Association, he organized conferences and conventions from 1991 through 1995. He edited fourteen of their ABA birdfinding guides from 1990 to 1997. From late 1997 to early 2002 Paul edited *Birding*, ABA's bimonthly magazine. He then served as ABA's director of conservation and public policy until late 2003. Paul next worked for Swarovski Birding, a North American birding project, and more recently for the National Wildlife Refuge Association, promoting support for our unique refuge system. He has served as a consultant to the refuge system on issues of birder visitation. Paul's concerns include an interest in bird conservation, shade-grown and bird-compatible coffee, and the breeding biology of North American birds. In this last regard, he coauthored (with the late Colin Harrison) *A Guide to the Nests, Eggs, and Nestlings of North American Birds.* Paul also has co-led a number of birding tours to the Aleutians, the Pribilofs, the Seward Peninsula, and St. Lawrence Island in Alaska. He serves on the Management Board of the Prairie Pothole Joint Venture, and on the Waterbird Conservation Council.

IF YOU GO

➤ **Getting There:** Corpus Christi is served by Continental and Delta; Harlingen is served by Continental, Southwest, and Sun Country; McAllen is served by American and Continental.

➤ **Best Time to Visit:** Birders will visit in the spring to coincide with northward migrations, the fall to coincide with southward migrations, and the winter to encounter a Mexican rarity. The Rio Grande Valley Birding Festival is held each year in November.

➤ **Guides:** Many birding-tour companies lead trips to the Lower Rio Grande Valley, including Victor Emanuel Nature Tours (800-328-8368; www.ventbirds.com) and Wings Birding Tours (888-293-6443; wingsbirds.com). The World Birding Center (956-584-9156; www.worldbirding center.org) has excellent resources for do-it-yourselfers; The Great Texas Coastal Birding Trails, sponsored by the Texas Parks & Wildlife Department (www.tpwd.state.tx.us) is also useful.

➤ **Accommodations:** McAllen is central to the valley, and the McAllen Chamber of Commerce (956-682-2871; www.mcallen.org) lists lodging options here. The Harlingen Chamber of Commerce (800-531-7346; www.harlingen.com) lists lodgings in Harlingen.

CARONI LAGOON

RECOMMENDED BY **Clay Taylor**

"A lot of enthusiastic new birders decide that they need to go and experience the rain forest—Costa Rica, Ecuador, etc.," Clay Taylor began. "They go down to those places, and without a guide, they get horribly frustrated. The dense vegetation only allows them a quick glimpse of a bird, and then their bird book shows six or eight bird species that appear identical to what they saw. It's tough for someone who's used to birding around Boston to go down there and have success. I like to think of Trinidad as 'Tropical Birding 101.' All the families of South American bird species are represented there. You can get a feel of how to find antbirds and trogons and other species, without suffering a bad case of field-guide shock. From a logistical perspective, it's also very comfortable. Trinidadians speak excellent English, the water is potable, and there are no worries about malaria. They do drive British, but you can still make your way around easily."

The Republic of Trinidad and Tobago is a small island nation (roughly 2,000 square miles) in the southern Caribbean, just northeast of Venezuela. Trinidad is the far larger of the two islands, holds most of the republic's population, and is the focal point for most birding expeditions (though some of the republic's recorded species occur only on Tobago). Thanks in large part to their proximity to the South American continent, Trinidad and Tobago boast over 450 bird species. Two venues leap out as must-visits for anyone voyaging to Trinidad: Caroni Lagoon and the Asa Wright Nature Center.

Caroni Lagoon National Park and Bird Sanctuary is a twenty-one-square-mile mangrove swamp thirty minutes south of the republic's capital of Port of Spain. It's regarded as one of the Western Hemisphere's most intact mangrove ecosystems, and is home to marine possums, tree boas, mongoose, caiman, crab-eating raccoons, and 160 species of birds—including thousands of Scarlet Ibises. That any of these flaming-red icons exist in Caroni at all is a small miracle, and testimony to the determination of a local naturalist named Winston Nanan.

DESTINATION

45

For much of the past century, hunters have blasted away at Caroni's ibises, as their feathers are prized for hats and carnival costumes. A small refuge established within the swamp in 1948 (with the help of Winston's father, Simon) did little to protect the birds. Poaching persisted even after Trinidad and Tobago declared their independence from Great Britain in 1962 and named the Scarlet Ibis their national bird, and by the mid-seventies, ibises were no longer nesting in Caroni. It was at this time that Winston Nanan began to publicly voice his outrage at the lack of oversight and animal protection in the swamp. Birdwatchers internationally and local residents alike rallied around Nanan at what increasingly appeared as an affront to a national treasure. The government eventually took action, naming Caroni a national park and escalating warden presence. By the early nineties, ibises began nesting again in Caroni. Poaching has not been completely eliminated and increasing salinity in the marsh poses ecological challenges, but today it's estimated that some 2,500 Scarlet Ibises again nest in Caroni, drawing cruise-ship transients and more dedicated avian enthusiasts alike.

The seminal Trinidadian birding event can be experienced each day at dusk at Caroni Lagoon, when the Scarlet Ibises come in to roost. "You can go out for a half- or full-day tour on the lagoon, or just for the sunset tour," Clay continued. "You'll get in a little boat and head up and down channels. You should be able to see boas and a host of birds. If you draw one of the better guides, they'll be able to provide an excellent history of the place. While the preamble is very enjoyable, everyone knows that the big event is still to come, and late afternoon builds to a crescendo. An hour before sunset, you'll moor up to some buoys. Soon after, the ibises begin flying in, brilliant red against a blue sky dotted with white thunderheads, the oranges of the setting sun glinting off the green of trees. I don't know of any place else where you can experience such a spectacle."

The Asa Wright Nature Center rests in the modest mountains of Trinidad's Northern Range, a few hours north of Port of Spain. While less likely to attract cruise shippers, it's a must-stop for birders who make it to the island. "You need to stay here at least a day or two," Clay continued. "The birding is excellent, and you get a very strong sense of the British influence on Trinidad— they even serve a tea!" The center—which has in the past been recognized by *Audubon* magazine as one of "The World's Ultimate Outposts"—consists of 1,500 forested acres in the Arima and Aripo Valleys, and includes accommodations and extensive exhibits. (Asa Wright is considered the Caribbean's first ecotourism operation, and a model for future ecolodges.)

The area gained notoriety in the 1930s when William Beebe (of the New York Zoological Society) established a field station (Simla Nature Center) here to study New World tropical birds.

OPPOSITE: Scarlet Ibis are the national bird of Trinidad and Tobago.

DESTINATION 45

This, and the presence of a cave that hosted Oilbirds on the adjacent property that eventually was purchased by Newcombe and Asa Wright, brought ornithologists from far and wide to the Arima and Aripo valleys. A colony of over 150 *guachoros* reside in Dunston Cave, considered one of the most accessible places anywhere to witness these nocturnal creatures, which navigate by echolocation. Today, among Asa Wright's many attractions—Ornate Hawk Eagles, Golden-headed Manakins, and Bearded Bellbirds, for starters—the Oilbirds continue to be a standout.

CLAY TAYLOR is a Connecticut Yankee; he resides in Moodus, Connecticut, with his wife, Debbie, and a son, Jonathan, and daughter, Grace. He grew up roaming the woods of Connecticut, collecting butterflies, rocks, etc., and doing the kinds of things kids like to do outdoors. Clay became interested in photography in the 1970s while attending college in Rochester, New York, and that led to bird photography and birding in 1975. After college, he started leading bird tours, including his first of many trips to Trinidad in 1984. He also worked from 1983 to 1989 banding migrating hawks in Connecticut in the fall and New York in the spring; his work led to the founding of the Rochester Hawk Banding Project, which later became the Braddock Bay Raptor Research. Butterflies reentered the picture in 1994, when Clay was elected the founding president of the Connecticut Butterfly Association. In 1999, he was hired by Swarovski Optik N.A. (www.swarovski.com) as their birdwatcher, digiscoper, and naturalist market manager.

IF YOU GO

➤ **Getting There:** Port of Spain, Trinidad, is served by many major carriers, including American, Continental, and United. From Port of Spain, Caroni Swamp is roughly twenty-five miles south.

➤ **Best Time to Visit:** January through May and October are the driest months in Trinidad, though good birding can be had throughout the year.

➤ **Guides:** Many tour companies lead trips to Trinidad and Tobago, including Field Guides (800-728-4953; www.fieldguides.com), Victor Emanuel Nature Tours (800-328-8368; www.vent birds.com), and Wings Birding Tours (888-293-6443; www.wingsbirds.com). David Rooks Nature Tours (868-631-1630; www.rookstobago.com) is locally based.

➤ **Accommodations:** Asa Wright Nature Center (800-426-7781; www.asawright.org) and Pax Guesthouse (868-662-4084; www.paxguesthouse.com) are favorite lodging spots for birders.

SOUTH GEORGIA ISLAND

RECOMMENDED BY **Victor Emanuel**

Victor Emanuel has made much of his formidable birding reputation in the steamy southern climates of Mexico, Panama, and Peru. But a venue a good deal farther south, in somewhat less clement surroundings, has captured his imagination: South Georgia Island. "In terms of total wildlife and overall birding spectacle and diversity, South Georgia is the ideal place in the Antarctic," Victor began. "Indeed, I think that South Georgia ranks right up there with the Serengeti as one of the top wildlife spectacles in the world. The sheer numbers of King Penguins, Skuas, Elephant Seals, and Fur Seals—plus the backdrop of the mountains and the sounds and smells of the menagerie—are simply staggering. After visiting South Georgia on several occasions, I can understand why Roger Tory Peterson considered it one of his favorite places."

South Georgia is one of the most isolated island collections in the world. It rests nearly 1,300 miles east of Tierra del Fuego, and some 800 miles east of the Falkland Islands, on the same latitudinal line as Cape Horn. The island is long and narrow, roughly a hundred miles long and alternating from just one mile to twenty-five miles in width. Several mountain ranges extend along its center, namely the Allardyce and Salvesen, which include eleven peaks greater than 6,500 feet. During the island's brief summer, most of the ground remains cloaked in glaciers, ice caps, and snowfields; icebergs dot the coastline. The first European to view South Georgia was a London merchant named Antoine de la Roche, who took shelter near the island in 1675 after losing his way around Cape Horn. One hundred years later, Captain Cook came upon the island, thinking he had at last identified the last great continent. He was, of course, mistaken, and he named the island for King George. Cook's reports of great numbers of whales and seals in the waters around South Georgia brought first sealers and then whalers. The whaling onslaught began in earnest in the early 1900s. The world's greatest concentration of whales—Blue, Fin, Sei, Humpback, and Southern Right—were reduced to a mere 10 percent (or less) of their former populations. In 1974,

these species received protection under the International Whaling Convention, and their numbers are slowly increasing. The islands played a role in polar explorer Sir Ernest Shackleton's greatest adventure, when he a led a crew of five in an open boat from Elephant Island to South Georgia in 1915 after their expeditionary ship, the Endurance, was crushed by ice. On a later expedition, Shackleton died, and he is buried on the island at the old whaling station in Grytviken.

While not especially broad in species diversity (eighty-one bird species have been documented around the islands; en route from South America, another forty or so have been observed), South Georgia is home to some fascinating specimens. Several members of the penguin family—King, Gentoo, Adelíe, Macaroni, Chinstraps—are present in great numbers, with Kings breeding in overwhelming colonies. Birders will also treasure the opportunity to have close contact with several species of albatross. "Gray-headed Albatross breed at a place called Bird Island, and on Elsehul Bay," Victor continued. "On two occasions, I've been lucky enough to take a Zodiac into Bird Island and land. The huge numbers of fur seals that are often there were mostly gone, and we could climb up to the ridge to see the birds on their nests.

"At a place called Gold Harbor, there are nesting Light-mantled Albatross; South Georgia is one of the few places they breed. Gold Harbor is my favorite spot on South Georgia—there's a beautiful glacier, hills of tussock grass and snow-capped mountains in the distance, plus the requisite penguin colony and thousands of fur seals. For many albatross connoisseurs, the Light-mantled Albatross is a favorite. It's a graceful bird, with a particularly enchanting, haunting call that you wouldn't expect from a seabird. At Gold Harbor, they're gliding around at the ridge tops."

The bird with the world's largest wingspan—the Wandering Albatross—can also be found on South Georgia. Wandering Albatross range throughout the Southern Ocean, feeding on squid, small fish, and any animal refuse they can find near the surface. Their wingspans can reach over twelve feet, though ten feet is closer to the average. Rivaling Poe's raven in avian literary stature, the Wandering Albatross was immortalized in Samuel Taylor Coleridge's "The Rime of the Ancient Mariner." (The poem's protagonist is punished for shooting an albatross with his crossbow, and eventually compelled to wear the dead bird around his neck. Wandering Albatross, which would sometimes follow ships at sea for long periods, provided sailors with a level of companionship and hence were considered harbingers of good fortune.) "People can land on Prion Island on a controlled basis to see the birds on their nests," Victor said. "To see a pair of Wandering Albatross on their nest with eggs is one of the greatest sights any naturalist can experience."

The voyage to South Georgia Island demands a level of commitment. It's a long nautical journey, and the weather is not always agreeable. "On my first trip in November of 1981, we hit a

OPPOSITE: Visitors to South Georgia have the rare opportunity to see nesting Wandering Albatross.

DESTINATION

46

203

terrible storm," Victor recalled. "The weather was so bad, we weren't able to land. Five years later I returned, and we were able to land in many places. My first landing at Gold Harbor still stays with me. It was perfect day—little wind, mild temperatures, and bright sunshine, which brought out the colors on the penguins' heads. Albatross and kestrels were wheeling above and Elephant Seals were bellowing. I was completely immersed in the noise of the colony."

VICTOR EMANUEL started birding in Texas at the age of eight, and is the founder and president of Victor Emanuel Nature Tours (www.ventbird.com). His travels have taken him to all the continents, with his areas of concentration being Texas, Arizona, Mexico, Panama, and Peru. Victor is the founder and compiler for forty years of the record-breaking Freeport Christmas Bird Count, and served a term as president of the Texas Ornithological Society. Birds and natural history have been a major focus throughout his life. Victor initiated the first birding camps for young people, and considers that one of his greatest achievements. He holds a B.A. in zoology and botany from the University of Texas and an M.A. in government from Harvard. In 1993, he was the recipient of the Roger Tory Peterson Excellence in Birding Award, given by the Houston Audubon Society in recognition of a lifetime of dedication to careful observation, education, and addition to the body of ornithological knowledge. In 2004, Victor received the Roger Tory Peterson Award from the American Birding Association, and the Arthur A. Allen Award from the Cornell Laboratory of Ornithology. He is on the boards of the Cornell Laboratory of Ornithology and the American Bird Conservancy.

IF YOU GO

► **Getting There:** Birding tours to South Georgia Island (which generally include stays at Antarctica and/or the Falkland Islands) depart from southern Argentina from several ports, including Puerto Madryn (reached via the airport at Trelew) and Ushuaia; both cities are served by Aerolineas Argentinas via Buenos Aires.

► **Best Time to Visit:** The window for visiting South Georgia and Antarctica is in the Southern Hemisphere summer; most trips depart from late December through January.

► **Guides/Accommodations:** Birders will need to join a tour to visit isolated South Georgia. Several companies visit the island, including Victor Emanuel Nature Tours (800-328-8368; www.ventbirds.com) and Wings Birding Tours (888-293-6443; www.wingsbirds.com).

THE SILK ROAD

RECOMMENDED BY **Steve Rooke**

For more than 1,500 years, the Silk Road connected East and West, fostering trade and laying the groundwork for the development of civilizations along its route, from China to Rome. Myriad fortunes were made along its byways (the Silk Road was actually not one road, but a series of interconnected routes). Very different riches await birders today—a chance to observe a number of endemic species against a backdrop of rich, and very much preserved, history. "I first went on what's become known as our Silk Road Tour in 1993," Steve Rooke began. "The countries we visited—current-day Uzbekistan and Kazakhstan—were still part of the Soviet Union. There was something incredibly exciting about traveling to parts of the world that few outsiders had visited. I'd certainly heard about places like Tashkent, but didn't know very much, as these countries had been closed for so long. Now that these countries have their own identity, things have opened up much more. They're still fascinating places to visit."

Uzbekistan and Kazakhstan rest in the heart of central Asia, north of Afghanistan (and the other "stans"), northwest of China and southwest of the Russian Federation. Bordered by the Caspian Sea to the west and the Tien Shan mountains in the east, much of the habitat is harsh steppe, dotted with occasional oases of moisture and forest land. Steve's adventures have generally begun in Uzbekistan. "We'll spend some time in the cities of Samarkand and Bukhara," he continued. "Samarkand is the site of the Registan, a collection of madrassas that's among the more famous landmarks in central Asia. I find Bukhara even more interesting from a historical perspective, as a large chunk of the old town is still intact, waiting to be explored. Bukhara is home to the Kalen Minaret, one of the few buildings that Genghis Khan did not destroy when he sacked Bukhara. It dates back to the tenth century; legend has it that a fire was lit at the top so it would act as a lighthouse of sorts for the caravans coming across the desert." At Samarkand, the exotic birding wonders of Uzbekistan also begin to unfold. "Outside the city, we have found Eastern

DESTINATION

47

Rock Nuthatch, White-throated Robin, Eastern Orphean, and Upcher's Warblers, Red-backed Isabelline and Lesser Gray Shrikes, Hume's Short-toed Lark, and Asian Paradise Flycatchers," Steve added. "Near Bukhara, we might observe Ménétrie's Warblers, Blue-cheeked Bee-eaters, Pied Bush Chats, Rufous Bush Robins, smart Citrine Wagtails, noisy Sykes's Warblers, and White-tailed Plovers." From Bukhara, the Silk Road birding caravan veers west to the vast Kyzyl-Kum desert (which encompasses some 115,000 square miles), in search of the Pander's Ground Jay, one of the more sought-after Central Asian endemics. Little Owl and Streaked Scrub Warbler will also likely be found here.

After a rest stop in Tashkent, the caravan pushes east (by plane) to the city of Almaty and the beginning of the Kazakhstan segment of the tour. Kazakhstan is the eighth-largest country in the world, and boasts nearly 500 recorded bird species (and almost 400 breeding species). While it's impossible to cover the country in a week's time, Steve's group attempts to provide a survey that will reveal the most intriguing Kazakh species. First, the caravan makes its way east across desert plains cut with deep gorges, with the snow-capped Tian Shans looming in the distance. "This is great raptor country," Steve continued, "and we could see Saker, Golden, Imperial, and Steppe Eagles, as well as a small breeding colony of Himalayan Griffons. We should also see Gray-necked Buntings, Pallas's Sandgrouse, and Pale Martins before we head back to Almaty and then north to the Taukum Desert."

The Taukum Desert, a country of clay and sand hills, promises to transport visitors to a different time. "The landscape here has not changed much in hundreds, if not thousands of years," Steve said. "You half expect Genghis Khan and his Mongol hordes to come storming through. On the way into the Taukum, we'll stop at a lake where there's a large colony of Rose-colored Starlings. We set up camp near an artesian well, which draws a legion of larks—Calandra, Bimaculated, Greater, Lesser, and Short-toed Larks. We're also likely to encounter McQueen's Bustard here. A little north, along the Ili River and its stands of turanga trees, we'll come upon Yellow-eyed Stock Dove, White-winged Woodpecker, Azure and Turkestan Tits, and the beautiful Saxaul Sparrow."

Another short plane ride brings the group to the capital city of Astana and the northern steppe country, composed of broad, sweeping grasslands dotted with lakes. "Around the wetlands near town, we'll see White-winged Black Terns, Marsh Sandpipers, Paddyfield Warblers, and Great Bitterns," Steve continued. "Out on the steppe, we'll hope to encounter Dalmatian Pelican as well as Black Lark and White-winged Lark, two semimythical birds that are difficult to see anywhere else. It's a great thing to turn 360 degrees and see hundreds of Black Larks in their display flight."

OPPOSITE:
Citrine Wagtails are often observed outside Bukhara, in Uzbekistan.

DESTINATION

47

Near the conclusion of the Silk Road Tour, assembled birders will finally heed the call of the mountains that have been beckoning from the east. After flying back to Almaty, the caravan heads toward the Zailiysky Alatau mountains in pursuit of two final exclamation points—Ibisbills and Himalayan Snowcocks. "Kazakhstan is one of the best places in the world to see Ibisbills," Steve explained. "It's always a big 'want' bird on everyone's list, and you're pretty much guaranteed to see it in the mountains here. The Snowcocks will generally take a little more work to find, but their eerie calls will usually reveal them. Red-fronted Serins, Güldenstadt's Redstarts, Severtzov's Tit-Warblers, Lammergeiers, and Altai Accentors may also be encountered in this alpine habitat. After the barren deserts, the evergreen forests, snow-capped peaks, and masses of wildflowers of the mountains are a welcome change."

STEVE ROOKE worked for the RSPB as a reserve warden for thirteen years before leaving to become a Sunbird (www.sunbirdtours.co.uk) staff leader. At one point he was leading up to ten trips each year, but since becoming the managing director of Sunbird he spends most of his time running the Sunbird office. However, Steve still leads tours to his favorite destinations—currently Central Asia, South Africa, and Ethiopia. He has a wide range of interests outside of birdwatching, not least of which is cooking.

IF YOU GO

► **Getting There:** The Silk Road Tour begins in Tashkent, Uzbekistan, which is served by Aeroflot via Moscow. The tour ends in Almaty, Kazakhstan, which is served by Lufthansa (via Frankfurt) and Turkish Airlines (via Istanbul).

► **Best Time to Visit:** May is the best time to visit Central Asia, as the grip of winter will have passed, and the intense heat of summer will not yet have arrived.

► **Guides/Accommodations:** Steve Rooke's company, Sunbird Tours (+44 176-726-2522; www.sunbirdtours.co.uk), leads the "Silk Road" tour described here. Local tour leaders include Bird Watching in Uzbekistan (www.birdwatching-uzbekistan.com) and Kazakhstan Bird Tours (www.kazakhstanbirdtours.com).

THE LLANOS

RECOMMENDED BY **Steve Hilty**

As many people live farther and farther away from the countryside, there's an increasing tendency to idealize the lives of cowboys, and the open spaces where they ply their trade. America has the Great Plains, Argentina the Pampas, and Venezuela (and neighboring Colombia) has the Llanos. "I've traveled extensively in Colombia and Venezuela," Steve Hilty began, "and people there definitely have a romantic view of the place—though many have never actually been there. The Llanos are not very easy to access. But for those birders who make the effort, comfortable facilities, great food, and a taste of *hato* (a Venezuelan term meaning "large ranch") culture await . . . and more birds than you can ever imagine."

The Llanos are a vast stretch of grassland plains that stretch from the Orinoco River west to the Andes. In Venezuela alone, these savanna lands comprise more than 115,000 square miles, roughly one third of the country. There are higher plains closer to the Andes; the land rests at lower altitudes near the river. "At a glance, the Llanos might not look like the sort of habitat that would harbor lots of wildlife, but it does," Steve continued. "There aren't many people there, but those who do live in the region run cattle. It's my impression that the cattle and wildlife form a harmonious mix; at least, cattle raising does not seem detrimental to the wildlife. There are two seasons in the Llanos: wet and dry. The habitat changes significantly between the rainy season and the dry season. In the rainy season, the lowlands get inundated with water that drains down from the high plains and overflows from the streams. At this time the cattle have to be trucked out to higher ground. The other half of the year it's bone dry, blowing dust. Despite the rather trying conditions, the animal life is extremely rich. There are giant anteaters—if you see one, it's hard to tell whether they're coming or going. There are capaybara, which resemble a hundred-pound New York sewer rat. There are also anaconda, ocelot, jaguar, and the nearly extinct Orinoco Cayman, which grow to immense sizes. And there are waders and waterfowl in spectacular numbers, plus raptors, macaws, parrots, and much more."

The Llanos are remote, far removed from Venezuela's population centers. There weren't any roads leading into the region until profits from the oil boom of the 1970s helped fund one such thoroughfare. Still, the lack of any visitor infrastructure greatly limited the area's birding potential. Circumstances changed when several of the huge *hatos* recognized the possibilities of eco-tourism to both supplement their cash flow and give them added visibility. For Steve, two *hatos* stand out: Pinero and Cedral. "The two ranches are quite different, situated in different parts of the Llanos," Steve continued. "Pinero is in the high Llanos, which are not so subject to flooding. It's very picturesque, with a blend of grasslands, wetlands, forest, and even some mountainous terrain. You don't get the huge concentrations of bird life at Pinero that you will find at Cedral, but I'd say that 90 percent of the same species are represented at both places—including Agami Heron, and all seven species of ibis. You have a particularly good chance of seeing ocelots at Pinero; we'll go out at night with a spotlight to locate them."

Hato El Cedral is in the heart of the low plains area of the Llanos, and is more typical of the region's greater ecosystem than Pinero. While it may lack some of Pinero's geographic diversity, it more than compensates in terms of sheer biomass. "El Cedral may have the biggest spectacle of waterfowl and wading birds anywhere in South America," Steve opined. "Some of the scenes seem as though they were lifted right from the Pleistocene era. (El Cedral's visceral appeal is not lost on media professionals; BBC, National Geographic, and Discovery Channel have all filmed segments here.) El Cedral used to belong to the owners of King Ranch in Texas, and when they were here, they built a number of dikes to collect water in the rainy season. The dikes form immense, shallow lakes. As the water gradually drains out, it supports a broad band of green grass that follows the slowly drying lake for miles. This creates excellent conditions for open country species of all kinds, as well as raptors and capaybaras. In the dry season, the lake beds are a magnet for any bird associated with water."

The spectacle Steve describes begins quite early on a typical birding day at El Cedral. "During the dry season when the majority of birders visit El Cedral, it's very hot. People are generally up by five or five-fifteen—whether they want to be or not. That's because many water birds roost in the trees that surround the cabins. The most vocal of the group are the Buff-necked Ibis. Before dawn, they begin this chant that has an incredible volume. First a few chant, then dozens, then a hundred, or several hundred. People don't think of ibis as being very vocal, but this species certainly is. You'll see the later-risers in the group peering out their windows, rubbing their eyes, and wondering what the racket is.

"With the help of the ibis, we'll get out early to beat the heat. Near the lakes, we'll come upon massive groups of birds. I've seen 250,000 Whistling Ducks, tens of thousands of ibises. Once we've absorbed these staggering numbers, we'll look for rarities like the Zig Zag Heron. Visitors usually want to see anaconda, which are fairly common around El Cedral. These are the world's largest snakes, and can easily reach lengths of twenty feet. A couple years ago, we spotted a good-size specimen—about fifteen feet long—close to one of the dikes on the ranch. [Anacondas spend much of their time in the water.] We got out of the truck to have a closer look. The guests were thirty or forty feet away from the head of the snake, while the Venezuelan guide and driver stood just to its right; they weren't concerned, as the bigger snakes are sluggish. As they described the snake to the visitors, I went behind it and grabbed its tail to drag it out into the open a bit more. As soon as I did so, the snake lashed out at the men at its side, who happened to be the closest thing to its mouth.

"They didn't get bitten. However, they made it clear that I shouldn't do that again."

STEVE HILTY is the senior author of A Guide to the Birds of Colombia, and the recently published Birds of Venezuela, both by Princeton University Press. Other credits include Birds of Tropical America, A Watcher's Introduction to Behavior, Breeding, and Diversity, which has just been republished by the University of Texas Press. He has also written a number of scientific papers on birds and plants, and is presently preparing the text and species accounts for the tanagers for a forthcoming volume of the acclaimed Handbook of Birds of the World, published by Lynx Press in Barcelona. Steve holds a Ph.D. in zoology from the University of Arizona and has worked at the Arid Lands Department at the University of Arizona, as a consultant to the Nature Conservancy, and as a stockbroker. He is currently a research associate at the University of Kansas Museum of Natural History. Since 1975, he has led tours throughout North and South America, and co-led trips to India, the Orient, and Australasian regions. With three decades of experience in South America and a wide range of natural history interests, he brings a unique breadth of expertise to his neotropical tours. At night he often turns his binoculars toward the skies for stargazing. Steve lives in Kansas City with his wife, Beverly. They have two college-age daughters.

► **Getting There:** To reach Hato Piñero, visitors fly into Caracas, which is served by many carriers, including Avianca, American, and Continental. To reach El Cedral, visitors fly into Barinhas, which is served via Caracas by Avior and Conviasa Airlines. Transfers from the airport to the *hatos* are provided.

► **Best Time to Visit:** Birders tend to favor the dryer winter months—November to April. This is especially true for El Cedral, which lies in lower country, and subsequently floods (though the arrival of the rainy season in late spring often stimulates much bird activity).

► **Guides:** Most major birding-tour companies lead trips that either focus on the Llanos or include a stay there as part of a Venezuela survey trip. Local guides are also available at the *hatos*.

► **Accommodations:** The two *hatos* favored by most birders visiting the Llanos are Piñero (+58 2-991-8935; www.hatopinero.com) and El Cedral (+58 212-781-8995; www.elcedral.com).

NECEDAH NATIONAL WILDLIFE REFUGE

RECOMMENDED BY **Joseph Duff**

Most birders ply their pastime by visiting places where birds nest, or at least are likely to pass through. Joe Duff goes one step further. He actually flies with the birds that he cares so passionately about—Whooping Cranes.

"I first got involved with using ultralight aircraft and human-led bird migration in 1993 with a fellow named Bill Lishman," Joe began. "Bill was the first person to fly with birds and was a sculptor and I was a photographer, and we were both looking for new adventures. We successfully led eighteen Canada Geese from Ontario to Virginia. We then formed Operation Migration (the nonprofit devoted to human-led migration efforts), and helped with the making of Fly Away Home, a feature film based on the first migration effort; actor Jeff Daniels portrayed Bill Lishman. Over the next few years, we found that Sandhill Cranes were amenable to ultralight-led migrations, as were Trumpeter Swans. [The birds are trained to recognize the pilots as a kind of mother figure from an early age, and are thus willing to follow them into the air.] We thought the idea could work with Whooping Cranes, and approached the International Whooping Crane Recovery Team. The recovery team had established a nonmigratory population in Florida, and was interested in establishing a migratory flock. They liked the Operation Migration concept and took it to the U.S. Fish and Wildlife Service, who also liked the idea, and began searching for the best possible locations for the new flock. They settled on Chassahowitzka National Wildlife Refuge in western Florida as the wintering location, and Necedah National Wildlife Refuge in central Wisconsin as the northern terminus, with Operation Migration's ultralight plane-led migration technique as the main reintroduction method."

Necedah National Wildlife Refuge is a 44,000-acre preserve situated in the Great Central Wisconsin Swamp, the largest wetland bog in the state, and home of Wisconsin's largest remaining oak savanna forest. "There used to be a million acres of this forest," Joe continued, "and it was

the breeding grounds for Passenger Pigeons. Now there's only 4,000 acres left. But overall, the area is excellent habitat. There are mixed forests and lots of clean water; the soil is so sandy that there hasn't been much farming in this area, hence there's no significant agricultural runoff. In addition to the preserve, there are 100,000 acres of adjacent protected habitat, and thousands of acres of cranberry bogs. There are Red-headed and Pileated Woodpeckers in the oak savanna, and Sandhill Cranes and other waterfowl in the wetlands.

"In addition to being the spring and summer home for the Whooping Cranes, Necedah provides habitat for endangered Massasauga Rattlesnakes and endangered Karner Blue Butterflies, and is the southernmost site for Timber Wolves. As a result, you have wolf-tracking teams, butterfly-counting teams, snake-monitoring teams, all driving around with rigs outfitted with fancy communications equipment. We used to joke with each other that we should have T-shirts made up with a graphic of a butterfly being eaten by a snake being chased by a crane being followed by a wolf. The caption would read: My endangered species is going to eat your endangered species!"

Whooping Cranes are the tallest birds in North America, at nearly five feet in height, and perhaps the best known of those species that teeter on the brink of extinction. Their name derives from their distinct cry, which rings especially clear on cool mornings in north country wetlands. Whooping Crane populations were never extremely robust in modern memory; it's believed that 1,400 birds were extant in 1860. By 1941, hunting and habitat loss had diminished the population to one last migrating flock of 15 cranes. The wild flock—which nests in Wood Buffalo National Park, straddling the border of Alberta and the Northwest Territories, and winters at the Aransas National Wildlife Refuge—has rebounded somewhat to approximately 225 animals. Combining the Wood Buffalo-Aransas flock, a nonmigratory flock that has been established at Kissimmee Prairie in Florida, and the Necedah-Florida flock, there are about 375 Whooping Cranes alive today.

Rearing young Whooping Cranes and educating them in the ways of migration and life in the wild is a complex and fascinating business. Joe Duff, who's quite capable of describing the process in intricate detail, painted the picture in broad strokes: "There are six Whooping Crane propagation centers, and the largest is the Patuxent Wildlife Research Center in Maryland. From the moment the birds pip, two sounds are played—that of an aircraft engine and a crane brood call. Once the birds hatch, they are moved from the brooder to indoor pens; in the wild, cranes lay two eggs, and one chick will often kill the other, hence the separation. When the chicks are eight to twelve days old, they're introduced to the ultralight aircraft. The brood call is used whenever we are near the birds. The birds eventually learn to follow the aircraft around

OPPOSITE: Whooping Cranes take flight behind Operation Migration's ultralight aircraft.

DESTINATION
49

215

as it taxis. It's important to mention that the limited number of humans that ever come in contact with the young birds are in costumes designed to disguise the human form—it's imperative that they never see humans or hear human voices or they will become imprinted on people and never be wild.

"Once their growth plates have closed—but before they've learned to fly—the birds are flown to Wisconsin, courtesy of Terry Kohler of Windway Capital. Once the birds have arrived, we taxi the planes, with the birds following them down the runway. Soon after, the planes will begin to fly, and the cranes aren't far behind. First they're running down the runway, then hopping, then flying short distances, then flying circuits. At this stage, it's important to begin introducing the three sets of birds that were raised so they make one cohesive flock. We have an observation deck at Necedah, and by mid-August we'll do passes with the aircraft and flock. Some days we'll have forty human observers. Once the birds have forty minutes of flying endurance, we're ready to set out for Florida. This occurs in mid-October.

"At first, it's difficult to get the birds to leave Necedah. Once they get out of sight of the refuge, they turn back. We found that by going a very short distance the first day (four miles) we can prevent them from turning back. The next day we go a little farther, then a little farther. Whooping Cranes fly at thirty-eight miles per hour. When we're migrating, we have four ultralight aircraft with the birds, just in case birds veer off, so we can bring them back. We get up to about 2,000 feet; the birds learn to fly in the vortices of our craft; the lead bird might only be six inches from our wingtip. On our best day we covered 200 miles in the course of a morning (we had a thirty-five-mile-per-hour tailwind). We were so far ahead of the ground crew, we had to relay messages to them."

In seven years of Necedah-to-Florida flights, Operation Migration and the Whooping Crane Eastern Partnership have introduced 62 birds into the east.

JOSEPH DUFF developed an early appreciation for nature and a love of flying while growing up in rural Ontario. Eventually, he earned his pilot's license while working in the Yukon Territories. Joe was one of Canada's leading commercial photographers, known primarily for his work with the world's major automobile manufacturers. After twenty years of running a studio in downtown Toronto, Joe joined Bill Lishman in 1993 and helped conduct the first human-led bird migration, and soon after cofounded Operation Migration (www.operationmigration.org). Since then, he has developed a keen interest in the science of migration and crane behavior, and no doubt has accumulated more hours in flight alongside more species of birds than any other human. Recently,

Joe led a team of pilots that conducted an aerial survey in search of the elusive Ivory-billed Woodpecker in Arkansas and Louisiana. His aircraft went on permanent display in the Smithsonian National Air and Space Museum in 2007. Joe and his wife, Diana, have one daughter, Alex. The family lives in the small town of Port Perry, Ontario, the home of Operation Migration.

IF YOU GO

➤ **Getting There:** Necedah is approximately 160 miles from Milwaukee, which is served by most major carriers.

➤ **Best Time to Visit:** Operation Migration and the Whooping Cranes under their tutelage are in full training mode from mid-summer through the end of September; the birds depart for Florida in early to mid-October. The Whooping Crane and Wildlife Festival in mid-September celebrates the birds' pending migration.

➤ **Guides:** Visitors may observe Whooping Cranes in flight training from an observation tower at Necedah. The Necedah National Wildlife Refuge (www.fws.gov/midwest/Necedah) has materials for self-guided tours of the refuge.

➤ **Accommodations:** The website of the annual Whooping Crane and Wildlife Festival (www.whooping-crane-festival.com) lists accommodations around Necedah.

DESTINATION

49

YELLOWSTONE NATIONAL PARK

RECOMMENDED BY **Terry McEneaney**

Terry McEneaney encourages birders to visit Yellowstone. But he wants them to know what to expect before they arrive. "Yellowstone National Park is not one of the hotspots in North America for watching a great diversity of birdlife," Terry began. "But it does offer an array of birds unique to this area of North America—and more important, a chance to see these birds in the context of 'ecology in action.' When I show people Yellowstone avifauna, I try to emphasize ecology—how the birds fit into the whole system—over the bland form of listing. I think the opportunity to show this 'big picture' is what differentiates the Yellowstone birding experience from other birding experiences."

Tucked into the northwest corner of Wyoming and spilling over into parts of Montana and Idaho, Yellowstone was the world's first national park, and thanks at least in part to its "Jellystone" characterization in Yogi Bear cartoons, is the country's best known and most beloved refuge. Yellowstone encompasses 3,400 square miles of forest, grassland, and wetland terrain, most of which rests at an altitude above 7,500 feet; this makes for often harsh conditions for its denizens. Yellowstone is synonymous with large mammals—moose, elk, bison, bighorn sheep, black bear, and, most pointedly, Grizzly Bear, wolves, and mountain lion. Certainly, the park's remote backcountry—seldom visited by any but the most adventurous humans—is one of the largest tracts of the kind of pristine habitat these animals need to thrive left in the lower forty-eight. For Terry, it's the park's unique geothermal properties—over 10,000 geysers, hot springs, mudpots, and fumaroles—that characterize the area. (Two-thirds of the world's geysers are found here!) These features are most obvious in the dead of winter. "The lack of people and the backdrop of snow and cold accentuate the geothermal activity," Terry continued. "With the steam and the snow and the sunshine, it's a wonderland. The wildlife are also more concentrated in the winter. There's not as much variety—over a few days, you're likely to see forty species of birds and twelve species of

OPPOSITE:

Yellowstone gives birders a chance to appreciate bird life in the context of a very intact—and very beautiful—ecosystem.

mammals—but there are large numbers of the wildlife present. When you come upon an ungulate carcass around one of the fumaroles or geysers, you see the complex ecological system at work. In addition to the wolves or coyotes that might be on the carcass, there will be eagles and ravens gathering around—perhaps other species as well."

Despite the short spring and summer season and the potential for snow at almost any time, a total of 323 birds have been documented in the park since 1872. "We have a total of 160 nesting species," Terry said, "with forty resident species that endure the snow and cold of the winter." Trumpeter Swan, the largest native North American waterfowl, are one species that toughs out four seasons in the park. Many will spy Trumpeters from Fishing Bridge along the northern shore of Yellowstone Lake or along the Yellowstone River in winter, long a favored spot for birders. Recognized from afar by their namesake call, Trumpeter Swans are among the park's most imperiled birds, with resident populations currently at less than 20 individuals. It's worth noting that Trumpeters played a serendipitous role in bringing Terry to Yellowstone. "I first came here in 1968 (from New Hampshire), and my most vivid birding memory of that trip was seeing a Trumpeter Swan on Beaver Lake in Yellowstone," he explained. "After finishing college at the University of Montana, I took a number of jobs with the park service throughout the West—assignments that no one else was particularly interested in taking—thinking that perhaps some day I'd make it back to Yellowstone. Some years later, I landed a position at Red Rocks Lake National Wildlife Refuge, not far from West Yellowstone, Montana. The park service invited me to give a talk on Trumpeter Swans. After the talk, the chief ranger asked if I would like to work at Yellowstone. That was twenty-six years ago.

"I like to think that it's not a coincidence that Yellowstone was dedicated on the same date as my birthday!"

The Great Gray Owl is the largest owl in North America, and one of Yellowstone's more enigmatic avian inhabitants. Though it's estimated that there are in the vicinity of a hundred pairs in the park, they are seldom seen. When there's a report of a Great Gray Owl, it's Terry McEneaney's duty to verify the sighting. Such a validation led to one of his favorite Yellowstone birding tales: "We had a report of a Great Gray Owl with owlets out in a Lodgepole Pine stump on the Yellowstone Plateau. The observers had given pretty precise directions. When I got to the spot they'd mapped out, I didn't see anything. Suddenly I noticed a Great Gray Owl swooping at something on the ground. I didn't think too much of it; the visitor had been correct. But as I looked on, the owl continued swooping down toward the ground, then landing back up on its perch. This appeared to be odd behavior, and I focused my binoculars a little more closely. Soon

I noticed that there was a pine marten running back and forth on a log; every time the marten went one way or another, the owl swooped down taking hairs off the marten's back.

"I thought it would be neat if I could witness the owl killing the pine marten; I don't think anything like that had been documented before. I said to myself, 'Don't move! Don't blow this observation!' I was about 150 yards away, so I sat down with my rear on the ground and my binoculars resting on my knees. I should also mention that I had baggy pants on.

"As I looked on, I realized that the Great Gray Owl was no longer swooping at the log in the distance, but instead was flying in my direction. That's because the pine marten was coming my way, too. In the name of science, I stayed still. 'Hang in there,' I told myself. Now they were only one hundred yards away, then fifty, then twenty-five. At this point, the pine marten had gone out of focus, the owl was coming at me full blast, and I was getting nervous. Sure enough, the pine marten ran right up my pants leg. With the owl bearing down on me and the marten heading toward my crotch, I jumped up and shook the marten out before it became too settled. At the last possible moment, the owl veered away. The last thing I saw was the pine marten running down the hill, with the Great Gray Owl still in hot pursuit, trying to take the hair off the marten's back."

TERRY McENEANEY is the staff ornithologist for Yellowstone National Park. Prior to this he was a biologist at Red Rock Lakes National Wildlife Refuge. He has more than thirty years' experience in the Greater Yellowstone area, has authored three books (Birds of Yellowstone, Birding Montana, and The Uncommon Loon), and has been a member of both the Montana and Wyoming Bird Records Committees. Terry has also written numerous scientific and popular articles, and has appeared in or has had articles in National Geographic, Birding, North American Birds, Living Bird Quarterly, Yellowstone Science, and Smithsonian magazines. He has been a field consultant for Nature, BBC's David Attenborough's Life of Birds series, National Geographic, and Audubon. Terry is an instructor of bird courses at the Yellowstone Institute and the Institute for Field Ornithology, and a trip leader for Field Guides. In addition, he teaches bird workshops to Yellowstone park rangers, interpreters, and tour guides. Terry has guided ornithologists/birdwatchers from all over the world, and his knowledge of the area and its birdlife is unparalleled.

IF YOU GO

➤ **Getting There:** Flights are available into West Yellowstone (served by SkyWest), at the western border of the park, and Bozeman (served by Alaska Airlines, Delta, and Northwest), roughly two hours from the park's west entrance.

➤ **Best Time to Visit:** There are more bird species present in Yellowstone's brief spring and summer, though there are opportunities to see the ecosystem in action year-round.

➤ **Guides:** Terry McEneaney leads tours in Yellowstone—especially in the winter—through Raven Idiot Bird Guide Adventure Services (406-848-7942; www.ravenidiot.com).

➤ **Accommodations:** The West Yellowstone Chamber of Commerce (406-646-7701; www.west yellowstonechamber.com/lodging) has a comprehensive list of lodgings. For information about accommodations and camping in the park, contact Yellowstone National Park Lodges (307-344-7311; www.nps.gov/yell).

DESTINATION

50

Editor: Jennifer Levesque
Designers: Galen Smith and Liam Flanagan
Production Manager: Jacquie Poirier

Fifty Places series design by Paul G. Wagner.

The text of this book was composed in Interstate and Seria.